2002

Merry Christmas Randel!

I hope we can cook up some yummy tarts with this book - Should be easy with you! XOXO Sandra

French Tarts

Tarts 101: the Basics

THE BOTTOM LINE: CREATING PERFECT CRUSTS

No matter how succulent, fragrant, and delicious the filling, no tart can be a great tart with a mediocre crust. As essential as a masterly foundation is to a well-built house, a fine crust crafted from top ingredients is crucial to the creation of a memorable tart. Before the advent of the food processor, making a crust from scratch was a bit of a chore, slowly working the dry ingredients into the wet ingredients with the fingertips until the dough reached the consistency of a thick paste—whence the French word for pastry dough, *une pâte*, and indeed for pastry, *pâtisserie*, derives. For most crusts, the food processor has transformed this procedure into a 15-second exercise accomplished by pressing a button.

There are many variations on the crust theme in a French cook's repertoire, but with one or two exceptions they are all based on flour and butter, with a liquid—water, milk, or eggs—to bind them. The most basic crust, a *pâte brisée*, a short-crust pastry, is simply the combination of flour, salt, butter, and a bit of water. Other crusts—

pâte feuilletée, *pâte brisée au sucre*, *pâte sucrée*, and *pâte sablée* among them—build on the basic formula, adding more butter, milk, cream, eggs, and sugar to create a base ideally suited to the filling. Some savory tarts call for a breadlike yeast dough, or olive oil instead of butter, some sweet tarts for a streusel or a meringuelike base.

I include a variety of crust recipes here, because even subtle variations in the crust's composition make a notable difference in the taste and texture of the crust, and thus the tart. While precise recipes for different types of crusts vary from chef to chef, I have developed a core group of crust recipes that are simple and dependable, which I include in the next chapter for easy reference, rather than having directions for each chef's crust with every tart recipe. In the rare instances where the crust called for in a tart recipe is truly unusual, such as Gérard Mulot's chocolate crust (page 104) or Michel Husser's crunchy streusel crust (page 80), the recipe accompanies the tart recipe.

Tarts 101: the Basics

Acknowledgments

The pleasure of doing this book was greatly enhanced by all the people who participated in its creation. I am deeply grateful to my agents, Gayle Benderoff and Deborah Geltman, and to my publishers, Leslie Stoker and Peter Workman, for making this book a reality. I also want to express my appreciation to my editor, Siobhán McGowan, to art director Jim Wageman, to designers Renée Khatami, Alexandra Maldonado, and Pat Tan, and to all of the talented team at Artisan—Hope Koturo, Carole Berglie, Beth Wareham, and Felice Primeau—who worked on this book.

For his wonderful photographs and his friendship, thanks as always to Guy Bouchet; for his terrific, imaginative illustrations and calligraphy, my gratitude to Alain Vavro.

My deepest appreciation is due to all the people who so generously offered me their distinctive recipes, and to all of those, as well, who facilitated their acquisition: Patrick Arton, Danièle and René Bérard, Jean-Paul Bonin, Monica Bøye-Muller, Sylvie and Félicien Cador, Jacqueline Cedelle, Lisa de Cossé-Brissac, Jean-Pierre Courteau, Ella Degouy, François Delahaye, Alain Ducasse, Dominique Ferrière, Isabelle and Valérie Ganachaud, Joel Guillet, Mary Homi, Michel Husser, Dominique and Bernard Loiseau, Gérard Mulot, Anne and Fabrice Néel, François Payard, Guy Payard, Marie-Thérèse Perrin, Jean-Luc Poujauran, André Renard, Gilles Renaud, Caline and Georges Richard, Michel Rostang, André Soltner, Guillaume Sourrieu, and Hedwige and François de Valbray.

I want to offer my special thanks to the charter members of the "Katonah Tart-Tasting Committee"—Teresa and Leslie Scott, Alice Finley, JoAnn Trautmann, Elaine Cohen, Evelyn Finley, and Dan Farkas—whose taste buds, comments, and tart-making abilities were invaluable to me during the many months I spent testing recipes, and whose company made the whole experience so much more fun.

And finally, all my love and heartfelt gratitude to my husband, Steve, who never wavered in the face of what must have seemed an endless onslaught of tarts, and was always ready to tuck into the next one with gusto and good humor; and to my son, Ben, who was enormously helpful as my willing kitchen assistant, and showed particular aptitude in the apple-peeling and cherry-stoning departments. He will one day soon, I hope, grow to love tarts.

French Tarts presents fifty of the most delectable and distinctive tart recipes that I've gathered from top bakers and *pâtissiers*, from chefs at favorite inns, hotels, and restaurants, and from great home cooks as well. The recipes are almost equally divided between dessert tarts and savory tarts to serve as hors d'oeuvres, appetizers, or light main courses. Going by several names—*tartes*, *tourtes* (a covered tart), *quiches*, *pissaladières*—the featured tarts hail from many different regions: Provence, Alsace, Burgundy, the Côte d'Azur, Monte Carlo, Bordeaux, and, of course, Paris. While most are an accurate reflection of the cooking of the French capital and countryside today, a few are traditional family heirlooms, and one, dotted with butter and soaked with rum, was a favorite of the great gourmand Toulouse-Lautrec.

A variety of techniques accomplish the full repertoire of French tarts. Some are open-faced, others are covered with a top crust or a fluffy cap of meringue; some are filled before baking, others are filled afterwards; some are baked in tart molds or rings, others are baked "pizza style," with a flat, hand-molded crust; some have layers of *crème pâtissière*, or custard, between the crust and the fruit, others have nothing but a wash of butter or a dash of sugar between the rich crust and the topping. A couple of the most sophisticated tarts—a multilayered smoked salmon tartlet and a twice-baked chocolate meringue confection—brashly stretch the limits of the tart genre. Some tarts are more demanding than others, but the majority of featured recipes are easy and relatively quick to prepare. Each one to me is a memory, a story, and an experience. I present them to you with the hope that they bring you as much pleasure and satisfaction as they have brought me, my family, and my friends. *Bon appétit*!

Introduction

Glossy, vibrant with color, brazenly luscious and tempting, the French tart cries out for attention. From every window of every *pâtisserie* in France, a tart beckons. This quintessentially Gallic creation is an ultimately desirable treat available to any passerby for immediate gratification. Plainly, the French tart has no shame.

Nothing says French pastry more simply and more eloquently than a classic, beautiful tart, its sweet or savory filling glowingly fresh, its crust a warm embrace of golden, flaky pastry. Just a glance at a seductive tart behind the glass of the *pâtisserie* primes the mouth for the pleasures of its sensuous mélange of textures, silky and smooth at the top of the palate with the crust's delicate counterpoint of crunch.

In the course of writing seven books on France over the last nineteen years, I've come to know French *pâtisserie*, and the vast array of regional tarts that I especially love, quite well. I've bought them from beguiling *pâtisseries*, ordered them in auberges from Alsace to Provence and in the greatest Paris restaurants as well, stashed away the recipes when I've been able to obtain them, and made them at home for all kinds of parties—even a festive breakfast or two! As simple as it is in concept, the tart boasts an almost infinite variety of guises. A straightforward and unpretentious creation, it can be presented without frills on some occasions, dressed up and decked out on others. More than any other pastry, the tart is defined by the season, filled with *fraises des bois*—tiny, highly perfumed wild strawberries—in May and June; bright-hued raspberries, peaches, apricots, and plums in the summer; apples and pears in the autumn and throughout the winter, when the bakers' ovens are also turning out tarts of lemon or leek, rice custards, or hearty potato-and-cheese creations, dubbed *à la boulangère*. No other example of the *pâtissier's* or *boulanger's* art so accurately reflects the bounty of the seasonal marketplace.

Contents

*For my mother, with love; her perfect family dinners
while we were growing up are still an inspiration.*

Editor: Siobhán McGowan
Production director: Hope Koturo

page 2: Raspberry Tart with Caramelized Cream, page 93

Published in 1997 by Artisan,
a division of Workman Publishing Company, Inc.
708 Broadway
New York, NY 10003-9555

Library of Congress Cataloging-in-Publication Data

Dannenberg, Linda.
    French Tarts : 50 savory and sweet recipes / Linda
Dannenberg : photographs by Guy Bouchet : illustrations
by Vavro.
        p.   cm.
    Includes index.
    ISBN 1-885183-39-9
    1. Pies. I. Title.
TX773.D285 1997
641.8'652—DC21
                                                    96-47965
                                                    CIP

Printed in Singapore

10 9 8 7 6 5 4 3 2

Second Printing

French Tarts

50 Savory and Sweet Recipes

LINDA DANNENBERG

PHOTOGRAPHS BY GUY BOUCHET • ILLUSTRATIONS BY VAVRO

Artisan ▲ New York

FILLINGS AND TOPPINGS

There are almost as many fillings for French tarts as there are stars in the sky. Fruits, vegetables, meats, eggs, fish, poultry, cream, cheese, jams, sugar, and even, to my surprise, snails are married in an infinite variety of combinations, some as straightforward as a child's rendition of chopsticks, others as complex and ineffable as a Mozart concerto.

In many tarts, eggs beaten with milk or cream, and sometimes thickened with flour, hold the ingredients firm; in other tarts, the ingredients, usually fresh fruit, rest atop a fluffy cushion of sweet pastry cream flavored with vanilla, a liqueur, or almonds. Some rustic tarts anchor their fresh fruit, such as red grapes, with a thick jam or compote made of the same fruit. Several fruit tarts, pure and simple, have nothing between the fresh fruit and the crust but a sprinkling of sugar occasionally combined with a bit of instant tapioca. And then there is one of my favorite tarts, Toulouse-Lautrec's Butter-Rum Tart (page 102), that has nothing in it but a dusting of sugar, a few dots of butter, and a generous splash of rum. The permutations of crust, topping, and filling are limited only by your imagination.

GLAZES

Glazes made from jams or jellies are what give many beautiful tarts in *pâtisserie* windows their color and irresistible glow. The general rule for glazing tarts is that red jams or jellies, particularly red currant jelly, work best for tarts composed of what the French call *fruits rouges*—strawberries, raspberries, blueberries, blackberries, boysenberries, or huckleberries; apple jelly works nicely on apple tarts; and orange-hued jams or jellies, such as apricot or orange marmalade, work best on tarts with fruits from the yellow-orange-green family—bananas, oranges, kiwis, apricots, peaches, nectarines, green grapes, and yellow plums. Jam or jelly glazes are applied after a tart has cooked and cooled. Occasionally a sugar glaze of confectioners' sugar or a simple sugar syrup is sprinkled or brushed on before the end of the tart's baking time.

To give a burnished glow to the fluted edges of a crust or an entire top crust, such as the savory Tourte Vosgienne—the Alsatian Meat Tart on page 66—an egg wash of the beaten yolk, or the entire beaten egg, is brushed on before baking. A shining glaze will add personality and professional panache to the simplest tart.

EQUIPMENT: TOOLS OF THE TART MAKER'S TRADE

The proper baking equipment greatly simplifies and enhances the art and pleasure of making tarts. It is not necessary to have a kitchen entirely outfitted with French cookware, but having the precise tool for every task makes a difference.

Among the essential elements in the tart maker's kitchen are:

• A large butcher-block cutting board, about 2 feet square, for chopping and slicing fruits and vegetables, and for kneading bread-style doughs for savory tarts.

• A marble pastry slab, about 2 x 3 feet or 2 feet square, which stays cool and keeps dough cool when rolling it out.

• A heavy rolling pin of marble, steel, or wood, at least 12 to 14 inches long, with handles (or without if you are an experienced and adept baker) for neatly rolling out pastry dough into a thin, almost translucent disk.

• An assortment of mixing bowls in a variety of sizes and materials—stainless steel, glass, and ceramic bowls for the broad variety of mixing tasks that arise in tart making, and a large copper bowl perfect for whipping up fluffy, cloudlike egg whites.

• A dough scraper, in metal or plastic, for lifting and cutting dough.

• One or two slim metal spatulas, called "palette knives," with rounded tips for spreading fillings and loosening pastry dough; a sharp paring knife; a very sharp chef's knife for precision chopping and slicing; several leaf-shaped cookie cutters for decorating a tart with excess dough; and a pastry wheel for cutting and marking dough.

• Several hardwood mixing spoons, two rubber spatulas, and two well-made wire whisks in small and medium sizes, for mixing, beating, and scraping.

• A black, heavy-gauge steel baking sheet with sloping sides in a versatile 16 x 24-inch size.

• A dredger—a large jar or can with a perforated, screw-on top—for topping a tart with a dusting of confectioners' sugar.

• A wood-handled pastry brush with natural bristles for painting on glazes.

• Kitchen parchment paper, an indispensable, greaseproof paper for a variety of baking tasks, such as lining a baking sheet and protecting the top of a tart from over-browning in the oven.

• A selection of tart pans and pie dishes, ideally one of each of the following: one 9- or 9½-inch and one 10- to 11-inch tinned steel, removable-bottom tart pan with fluted sides; a 9-inch and a 10- to 11-inch heavy-gauge black steel, removable-bottom tart pan with fluted sides (black steel absorbs more heat and browns a crust faster than tinned steel and is perfect for tarts with short baking times); a 9-inch springform pan with straight 2-inch sides; a 10-inch glass pie dish; a 9-inch deep-dish glass casserole of range-to-oven tempered glass for baking a tart Tatin; six or eight 3- to 4-inch removable-bottom tinned-steel tartlet molds for making individual tarts; and a set of miniature tartlet molds in either the classic round or *barquette* (boat) shapes—at least 24 is practical—for making bite-size hors d'oeuvre tarts. All this said, if I could have only one tart pan, it would be my 10½-inch black steel, removable-bottom pan—the one I use most often.

One final point: The temperature of your kitchen is almost as important as having the proper equipment when you are baking tarts. Pastry kitchens in France, called *laboratoires*, are always kept quite cool, around 60°F or slightly lower, since it is easier and more effective to manipulate buttery dough when it is cool. The warmer the dough, the greater the chance it will stick or tear while you're working with it. When making tarts, try to keep your kitchen on the cool side and your pastry dough, and pastries at any stage of creation, away from any heat source.

✔ *For sources, see Appendix on page 123.*

Classic Crusts, Pastry Creams and Glazes

CLASSIC CRUST RECIPES

If your kitchen is cool, the dough has chilled, and your work surface and rolling pin are floured, you should have no trouble rolling out the dough and transferring it to the tart pan. If your dough tears or sticks to the rolling pin, it is either too warm or needs more flour, or both. Knead in a bit more flour, rechill the dough, and start again. Don't despair if the dough tears and you don't have time to rechill it: crusts can always be "patched" with a leftover bit of dough, with no loss of taste and allure and no one the wiser! If you have a bit of leftover dough and want to enhance your tart's presentation, roll out the excess dough and, using a small, leaf-shaped cookie cutter, cut out pastry leaves. Lay them around the rim of the tart, one slightly overlapping the other. Brush with a bit of egg glaze, then bake as directed.

Pâte Brisée
FLAKY SHORT-CRUST PASTRY

The *pâte brisée* is the simplest and most straightforward pastry crust, composed of just flour, butter, salt, and water. It is the perfect base for most savory hors d'oeuvre and appetizer tarts, and also works well with some sweet fruit tarts.

- 1 1/2 CUPS ALL-PURPOSE FLOUR
- 8 TABLESPOONS (1 STICK) UNSALTED BUTTER, CHILLED AND CUT INTO SMALL PIECES
- 1/2 TEASPOON SALT
- 4 TABLESPOONS ICE WATER

Combine the flour, butter, and salt in a food processor or mixing bowl. Process 10 to 12 seconds, or mash with your fingertips, until the mixture has a dry, crumbly texture resembling coarse cornmeal. Add the water to the mixture and pulse 12 to 14 times, or work together with your fingertips, just until the dough begins to hold together in a mass, but before it turns into a ball. (The crust can become tough if it is processed even a few seconds too long.) If the dough is too dry and dense, add 1 to 2 more tablespoons of water and pulse 2 or 3 times, or work with your fingertips.

Remove the dough from the mixing bowl, work it into a ball in your hands, then transfer it to a sheet of plastic wrap or wax paper. Flatten the dough into a neat, smooth disk, wrap, and refrigerate for at least 1 hour. (You can make this dough ahead of time and store it in the refrigerator for 2 to 3 days.) MAKES ONE 12-INCH CRUST

☞ For baking instructions, see page 20.

———

Pâte Brisée à l'Oeuf
FLAKY SHORT-CRUST EGG PASTRY

This is a slightly richer form of the basic *pâte brisée* recipe and can be used any time *pâte brisée* is called for.

- 1 1/2 CUPS ALL-PURPOSE FLOUR
- 8 TABLESPOONS (1 STICK) UNSALTED BUTTER, CHILLED AND CUT INTO SMALL PIECES
- 1/2 TEASPOON SALT
- 1 EGG, BEATEN
- 4 TABLESPOONS ICE WATER

Combine the flour, butter, and salt in a food processor or mixing bowl. Process 10 to 12 seconds, or mash with your fingertips, until the mixture has a dry, crumbly texture resembling coarse cornmeal. Add the egg and the water to the mixture and pulse 12 to 14 times, or work together with your fingertips, just until the dough begins to hold together in a mass, but before it turns into a ball. (The crust can become tough if it is processed even a few seconds too long.) If the dough is too dry and dense, add 1 to 2 more tablespoons of water and pulse 2 or 3 times, or work in with your fingertips.

Remove the dough from the mixing bowl, work it into a ball in your hands, then transfer it to a sheet of plastic wrap or wax paper. Flatten the dough into a neat, smooth disk, wrap, and refrigerate for at least 1 hour. MAKES ONE 12-INCH CRUST

☞ For baking instructions, see page 20.

———

Pâte Brisée au Sucre
SWEETENED SHORT-CRUST PASTRY

The *pâte brisée au sucre*, a sweeter, flakier version of the classic *pâte brisée*, works nicely in all sorts of dessert tarts. This recipe, calling for milk instead of water and just a touch of baking powder, is favored by several top *pâtissiers* in Paris.

- 1 1/2 CUPS ALL-PURPOSE FLOUR
- 8 TABLESPOONS (1 STICK) UNSALTED BUTTER, CHILLED AND CUT INTO SMALL BITS
- 1/4 TEASPOON SALT
- 1/8 TEASPOON BAKING POWDER
- 1/2 CUP SUGAR
- 4 TABLESPOONS (1/4 CUP) COLD MILK

Combine the flour, butter, salt, baking powder, and sugar in a food processor or a mixing bowl. Process 10 to 12 seconds, or mash with your fingertips, until the mixture has a dry, crumbly texture resembling coarse cornmeal. Add the milk to the mixture and pulse 10 to 12 times, or work together with your fingertips, just until the dough comes together in a smooth mass, but before it forms into a ball. If the dough is too dry, add another tablespoon of milk and pulse or mix for a couple of seconds.

Remove the dough from the bowl, and work it into a ball with your hands. If the dough is very sticky, adhering to your fingers, coat your palms with flour once or twice and work it into the dough. The dough should be malleable and a bit tacky, but should not stick to your hands. Transfer the dough onto a piece of plastic wrap or wax paper, press it into a flat disk, wrap it well, and

refrigerate for at least 1 hour. (This dough can be made well ahead and stored in the refrigerator for 2 to 3 days.) MAKES ONE 12-INCH CRUST

❧ *For baking instructions, see page 20.*

Pâte Sablée
RICH SUGAR PASTRY CRUST

As rich, sweet, and crunchy as a sugar cookie, this pastry crust is best for simple, fresh fruit tarts and tartlets—strawberry, raspberry, tropical fruits—and for jam tarts. I love to have a little *pâte sablée* left over to make into a few thin crisp cookies, some sprinkled with cinnamon and sugar, others topped with a dab of raspberry jam and dusted with confectioners' sugar.

- 12 TABLESPOONS (1 1/2 STICKS) UNSALTED BUTTER, CUT INTO BITS AND SLIGHTLY SOFTENED
- 1 CUP CONFECTIONERS' SUGAR
- 2 LARGE EGGS, BEATEN
- 1/2 TEASPOON VANILLA EXTRACT
- 2 TABLESPOONS GROUND BLANCHED ALMONDS (OPTIONAL)
- 1/2 TEASPOON SALT
- 2 CUPS ALL-PURPOSE FLOUR

Combine the butter, confectioners' sugar, eggs, vanilla, almonds if you wish, and salt in a food processor or a mixing bowl and process 5 to 7 seconds, until blended. Add the flour 1/2 cup at a time, pulsing 2 or 3 times, or mixing, after each addition, until the flour is blended and the dough just comes together. Do not let it form a ball. The dough should be soft and pliable, but not sticky. If the dough is sticky, add 2 more tablespoons of flour and process, or mix for a few seconds until blended.

Remove the dough from the bowl, knead it between your hands for about 1 minute, then press it into a flat disk and set it on a piece of plastic wrap or wax paper. Wrap the dough well and refrigerate for at least 1 hour or even overnight. MAKES ONE 14-INCH CRUST, OR TWO 9-INCH CRUSTS

❧ *For baking instructions, see page 20.*

———————

Pâte Sucrée
FLAKY SWEET PASTRY

The *pâte sucrée* is a sweet, sugary pastry, with a touch of crunchiness from the egg.

The dough is often used in fresh fruit tarts where the shell is prebaked, then filled with a pastry cream and topped with glistening fresh fruit.

- 1 3/4 CUPS ALL-PURPOSE FLOUR
- 8 TABLESPOONS (1 STICK) UNSALTED BUTTER, CHILLED AND CUT INTO SMALL BITS
- 1/2 CUP SUGAR
- 3 TABLESPOONS GROUND BLANCHED ALMONDS (OPTIONAL)
- 1/4 TEASPOON SALT
- 2 LARGE EGGS, BEATEN

Combine the flour, butter, sugar, almonds if you wish, and salt in a food processor or a mixing bowl. Process for about 12 seconds, or mash together with your fingertips, until the mixture is dry and crumbly, resembling coarse cornmeal. Add the eggs and pulse 14 or 15 times, or mix, until the dough comes together but before it forms a ball. (If the dough seems too sticky, sprinkle in a generous tablespoon of flour and pulse once or twice, or mix, until blended.)

Remove the dough, form it into a ball with your hands, set it on a piece of plastic wrap, and press into a flat disk. Wrap and refrigerate at least 1 hour, or overnight.

(This dough can be made up to 2 days ahead.) Makes one 14-inch crust

❧ *For baking instructions, see below.*

―――――

Pâte Sablée Salée
RICH SAVORY PASTRY CRUST

Buttery and delicious, wonderful with simple appetizer and main-course tarts that have mostly vegetables and no cream in the filling, this pastry crust was given to me by Hedwige de Valbray, the young *châtelaine* of the Château des Briottières, an aristocratic bed-and-breakfast in the pastoral countryside of the Anjou region.

- 2 CUPS ALL-PURPOSE FLOUR
- 12 TABLESPOONS (1 1/2 STICKS) UNSALTED BUTTER, CUT INTO BITS
- 1 TEASPOON SALT
- 2 LARGE EGGS, BEATEN

Combine the flour, butter, and salt in a food processor or mixing bowl. Process for 10 to 12 seconds, or mash together with your fingertips, until the mixture resembles coarse meal. Add the eggs and pulse 12 to 14 times, or mix with an electric beater, until the dough comes together but before it forms into a ball.

Remove the dough from the bowl, knead for a minute in your hands, shape it into a flat disk, and set it on a sheet of plastic wrap or wax paper. Wrap the dough and refrigerate at least 1 hour or overnight. Makes one 14-inch crust or two 9-inch crusts

❧ *For baking instructions, see below.*

―――――

PASTRY BAKING INSTRUCTIONS

For an unbaked tart shell: On a floured work surface, or on a work surface covered with plastic wrap that has been taped in place and then lightly floured, roll out the dough with a floured rolling pin into a large circle ⅛-inch thick and at least 3 inches wider than the size of the tart pan you are using. Cut out a circle of dough 3 inches wider than the size of your tart pan, using a pot cover, a plate, or an inverted tart pan as a guide. For example, for a 10½-inch tart pan, cut out a 13½-inch circle of dough. Transfer the pastry circle to a buttered tart pan and press the dough gently into the bottom and fluted sides. Trim the dough so that just ½ inch extends above the rim. Fold this extension over upon itself to create a doubled ¼-inch border above the rim. This will compensate for a bit of shrinkage from baking and make a sturdier crust. Flute the edges, prick the bottom of the pan, cover with plastic wrap, and refrigerate for 15 minutes.

For a partially baked tart shell: Preheat the oven to 375°F. Line the tart shell with aluminum foil, then fill to the brim with dried beans, rice, or baking weights. Bake in the center of the oven for 8 minutes, remove the baking weights and the foil, return to the oven and bake 2 more minutes. Remove to a wire rack to cool.

For a fully baked tart shell: Proceed as above until you remove the foil and the baking weights. Return the tart shell to the oven and bake for 15 to 20 minutes, until the shell is a light golden brown all over. Some ovens will brown the shell much more quickly than others. Remove to a wire rack and cool before filling.

———————

Pâte Feuilletée Rapide
QUICK PUFF PASTRY

This is a slightly shortened version of the classic *pâte feuilletée* recipe, but it still requires more time and effort than any other crust. The result, though, is lovely—a nice, buttery, light and flaky pastry. When preparing a *pâte feuilletée*, work in a cool (about 65°F) kitchen. Always work with chilled, but not frozen, puff pastry dough. When this dough begins to reach room temperature, it gets sticky and difficult to work with. Begin preparations at least 3 hours in advance.

- 2 CUPS ALL-PURPOSE FLOUR
- 1/2 CUP CAKE FLOUR
- 1 TEASPOON SALT
- 6 TABLESPOONS COLD MILK
- 6 TABLESPOONS ICE WATER
- 1/2 POUND (2 STICKS) PLUS 4 TABLESPOONS UNSALTED BUTTER, CUT INTO BITS AND CHILLED

Combine the flours and salt in the bowl of a food processor. Add the 4 tablespoons of butter to the flours. Process for 8 seconds. Add the milk and the water and pulse about 10 times, until the mixture forms large "crumbs". Remove from the processor and knead for a few seconds between your palms to form the dough into a ball. The dough should be soft and satiny, but not sticky. If the dough is sticky, dust your palms with flour and work it gently into the dough. Wrap the dough in plastic wrap and refrigerate for 1 hour.

The dough can be rolled out for the first time after it has chilled for at least an hour, but it can be chilled for up to 2 hours. Fifteen minutes before rolling out the dough, remove the ½ pound of butter from the refrigerator and set aside. Working with a floured rolling pin on a lightly floured work surface, ideally marble, roll out the dough into a rectangular shape about 7 inches wide and 15 inches long. Sprinkle half of the butter bits over two thirds the surface of the dough, working lengthwise, leaving a ½-inch border bare around the edges. Fold the unbuttered third over the center third of the dough, then fold the final third over the other two. Press down all open edges to seal the package like an envelope, with the sealed sides to your right and left. Turn the package ninety degrees so that the sealed sides are now on the top and bottom. Lightly re-flour the working surface and the rolling pin, and roll the dough out again to a 7 x 15-inch rectangle. Sprinkle the remaining butter over two thirds the surface, and fold again as before, the bare third over the center, the final third over that. Seal the edges, wrap snugly in plastic wrap, and chill for 1 hour.

Place the dough on a lightly floured work surface with the sealed sides on the top and bottom. Roll out the dough to three times its original size. Fold it in thirds like a letter, gently press it down with the rolling pin, then turn it ninety degrees. Re-flour the rolling pin and the work surface if necessary and roll the dough out again to three times its original size. Fold the dough in thirds, press it lightly with a rolling pin, wrap it tightly in plastic wrap, and refrigerate for at least 1 hour, or up to 2 days. It is now ready to use. Divide the dough in half for each single crust or four tartlet shells. MAKES TWO 10-INCH CRUSTS

ᵛ For baking instructions, see note below and directions on page 20.

and directions on page 20.

Note: For a partially baked tart shell, bake in the center of the oven for 10 minutes, remove the baking weights and the foil, and let cool.

PASTRY CREAMS

*T*he classic French pastry cream, *crème pâtissière*, acts as a delicate bond, marrying fresh fruit to a tart's crust or filling out the airy pastry pockets of eclairs and *religieuses*. *Crème anglaise*, a rich custard cream sauce, is the "ocean" that flows under *îles flottantes* (floating islands), as well as *charlottes*, bread puddings, and sponge cakes.

Crème Pâtissière
CLASSIC FRENCH PASTRY CREAM

This smooth and silky pastry cream is a versatile custard filling for tarts, puff pastries, and *choux* pastries such as eclairs. The basic cream is flavored with vanilla, but it also lends itself to variations such as chocolate, almond, and Grand Marnier creams.

- 1 1/2 CUPS MILK
- 1/2 VANILLA BEAN, SPLIT, OR 1 TEASPOON VANILLA EXTRACT
- 3 LARGE EGG YOLKS
- 1/4 CUP SUGAR
- 1 TABLESPOON CORNSTARCH
- 1 TABLESPOON FLOUR

In a heavy-bottomed saucepan, bring the milk to a boil over medium heat. If you are using a vanilla bean, add it now, cover the pan, remove it from the heat, and set aside. Combine the egg yolks and sugar in a glass or ceramic mixing bowl, then whisk briskly for about 2 minutes, until mixture is thick and pale yellow. Add the cornstarch and flour and whisk to blend. Remove the vanilla bean, if used, from the milk. If a skin has formed over the milk, remove it. Slowly pour the milk into the egg mixture, whisking until blended and smooth.

Return the mixture to the saucepan and bring to a boil, whisking constantly over medium heat. Reduce the heat to low and cook at a simmer, whisking constantly so that the bottom won't burn, for 2 minutes, until thick, smooth, and yellow. Remove from the heat and immediately strain the cream into a clean bowl. If you are using vanilla extract, stir it in now. Cover the cream with a sheet of plastic wrap placed directly on the surface of the cream to prevent a skin from forming. Cool, then refrigerate the cream for at least 1 hour, or even overnight. (Pastry cream can be made up to a day ahead and refrigerated.)

PASTRY CREAM VARIATIONS

For a lighter, airier pastry cream that is very nice in fresh fruit tarts: Whip 1 cup of heavy cream with ½ teaspoon vanilla extract and 1 tablespoon confectioners' sugar until firm peaks form. Fold the whipped cream into the finished, chilled pastry cream. Use in any recipe in place of the classic pastry cream.

For chocolate pastry cream: Melt 6 ounces bittersweet dark chocolate in a double boiler, then stir into the still-warm pastry cream. Chocolate pastry cream is used mainly as a filling for eclairs and cream puffs, but it makes a delicious and unusual base for a banana tart, or as a filling for tartlet shells topped with sliced strawberries.

For almond pastry cream: Stir in ⅔ cup finely ground blanched almonds and 3 tablespoons dark rum to the cooling pastry cream. Try it instead of classic pastry

cream in fruit tarts with plums, exotic fruits, or bananas.

For Grand Marnier pastry cream: Stir in 3 tablespoons Grand Marnier liqueur to the cooling pastry cream. Use in place of the classic pastry cream in strawberry or citrus tarts.

Crème Anglaise
VANILLA CREAM SAUCE

Although dubbed "English cream," *crème anglaise* has been an integral part of French cooking since the mid-nineteenth century. Traditionally it is flavored with vanilla, but for variety you can substitute 2 tablespoons of rum, Grand Marnier or kirsch for the teaspoon of vanilla. *Crème anglaise* is best served the day it's prepared, at room temperature, but it can also be refrigerated for a day or two and served chilled. It is an extremely versatile sauce that can embellish a variety of desserts, from fruit tarts and chocolate tarts to a simple plate of berries.

- 5 LARGE EGG YOLKS
- 1/2 CUP SUGAR
- 2 CUPS MILK
- 1 TEASPOON VANILLA EXTRACT

In a large saucepan, whisk together the yolks and the sugar. In another saucepan, heat the milk and the vanilla extract over medium heat until hot but not boiling. Pour the hot milk into the yolk mixture, stirring constantly with a spoon. Set over medium heat and stir constantly until the sauce thickens and coats the back of the spoon. Do not let the sauce come to a boil or it will curdle. Remove from the heat and place plastic wrap directly on the surface to prevent a skin from forming. Let cool, then refrigerate if not serving immediately. Serve separately in a sauceboat to accompany dessert tarts such as the Normandy Apple Tarts (page 74), the Alsatian Apple Streusel Tart (page 80), the Caramelized Apple-Meringue Tart (page 82), or the Pear Tartlets (page 86).

GLAZES

Most glazes, made from jam or jelly, are extremely simple to prepare. The basic recipes are given below. In the few instances where an unusual glaze is called for, the recipe appears along with the tart recipe.

APPLE JELLY GLAZE

• 1/2 CUP APPLE JELLY

Melt the jelly in a small saucepan over medium heat or in the microwave in a small microwavable dish. Remove from heat, then whisk until smooth. Apply the glaze with a pastry brush while still warm. If the glaze starts to thicken, add a tablespoon of water and reheat.

APRICOT JAM OR ORANGE MARMALADE GLAZE

- 1/2 CUP APRICOT JAM OR ORANGE MARMALADE
- 1 TABLESPOON KIRSCH OR FRESH LEMON JUICE

Melt the jam or marmalade in a small saucepan over medium heat, stirring occasionally. Remove from the heat, stir in the kirsch or lemon juice, and strain immediately into a small bowl. Apply the glaze with a pastry brush while still warm. If the glaze thickens, add a tablespoon of water and reheat.

RED CURRANT JELLY GLAZE

- 1/2 CUP RED CURRANT JELLY
- 1 TABLESPOON KIRSCH OR WATER

Melt the jelly in a small saucepan over medium heat, stirring occasionally. Remove from the heat and whisk in the kirsch or water until the mixture is blended and smooth. Apply the glaze with a pastry brush while still warm.

BASIC FRUIT TARTS

The majority of tarts that gleam from the windows of French *pâtisseries* are created from components described in this chapter—pastry crust, pastry cream, and a glaze drizzled atop fresh fruit. Such tarts are simple to make and very attractive to serve. Here are two recipes for basic fruit tarts, the first one filled with *crème pâtissière*, the second one—an even easier version—filled with *crème fraîche*.

BASIC FRUIT TART I

This tart can be filled with all kinds of fresh fruit—nectarines, oranges, litchis, melons. The recipe below is for a Tarte aux Fruits Exotiques. Another variation, made with seasonal berries and Red Currant Jelly Glaze (page 26), is shown on page 14.

- 1 10 1/2-INCH PÂTE SABLÉE SHELL (PAGE 18), FULLY BAKED
- 1 RECIPE CRÈME PÂTISSIÈRE (PAGE 23)
- 2 BANANAS, SLICED
- 2 KIWIS, PEELED AND SLICED THIN
- 1 MANGO, PEELED AND SLICED INTO STRIPS ABOUT 3 X 3/4 X 1/8-INCHES THICK
- 1 PERFECT LARGE STRAWBERRY, OR 1/4 CUP CHOPPED FRESH PINEAPPLE, FOR CENTER
- 1 RECIPE APRICOT GLAZE (PAGE 26)

Spread the pastry cream over the bottom of the tart shell. Arrange the fruit in concentric circles, starting at the outside edge with a ring of bananas, each slice slightly overlapping the other. Then make a circle of kiwis, again each slice overlapping the other. In the center of the tart, arrange the mango slices in the form of a daisy-like flower, each piece a "petal." Leave an open space of about 1½ inches in diameter in the very middle. Place the large strawberry, its leaves still intact, in the center, or fill with chopped pineapple. Brush the glaze over the fruit and chill for at least 1 hour before serving. SERVES 6 TO 8

BASIC FRUIT TART II

Refrigerate this tart for an hour or two before serving, so that the filling can slightly soften the crust. My favorite way to make this tart is with a mix of three berries—raspberries, strawberries, and blueberries—what the French call a Tarte aux Fruits Rouges.

- 1 10 1/2-INCH PÂTE SUCRÉE SHELL (PAGE 19), FULLY BAKED
- 1/4 CUP STRAWBERRY JAM
- 1 CUP CRÈME FRAÎCHE
- 1 CUP RASPBERRIES
- 1 CUP BLUEBERRIES
- 1 CUP STRAWBERRIES, SLICED IN HALF OR QUARTERED, DEPENDING ON SIZE
- 1 RECIPE RED CURRANT GLAZE (PAGE 26)
- 1/2 CUP TOASTED SHAVED ALMONDS

Spread the strawberry jam over the bottom of the tart shell. Spread the *crème fraîche* over the jam. Mix the berries together in a large bowl, then spoon into the tart shell over the *crème fraîche*. Drizzle the glaze over the berries, then scatter the almonds across the top to garnish. SERVES 6 TO 8

Savory Tarts

Tarte aux tomates et au prosciutto

TOMATO-PROSCIUTTO TART

- 1 RECIPE PÂTE FEUILLETÉE RAPIDE (PAGE 21), ROLLED OUT INTO SHEETS 1/8-INCH THICK, OR 2 SHEETS COMMERCIAL PUFF PASTRY, CHILLED BUT NOT FROZEN

- 3 GARLIC CLOVES

- 2/3 CUP OLIVE OIL

- 1/4 POUND PROSCIUTTO

- 1/2 TEASPOON FRESHLY GROUND BLACK PEPPER

- 10 FIRM, NICELY SHAPED PLUM TOMATOES, SLICED INTO 1/4-INCH ROUNDS

- 1 TEASPOON FRESH THYME

- 1/2 CUP LOOSELY PACKED FRESH BASIL LEAVES, FINELY CHOPPED

This rich and delectable tart draws raves every time I serve it. It comes from two-star Paris chef Michel Rostang, who created it for his popular bistro, the Bistro d'à Côté, built from turn-of-the-century elements right next door to his eponymous Michelin-starred establishment. Once you've prepared the required puff pastry dough, this colorful tart is easy and quick to make.

Preheat the oven to 375°F.

Roll out the dough to a thickness of ⅛ inch. Using a cereal bowl or a small pot cover as a guide, cut out six 4-inch circles. Grease a baking sheet, then transfer the dough circles to the sheet, spacing them evenly.

Combine the garlic, ⅓ cup of the olive oil, the prosciutto, and the pepper in the bowl of a food processor. Process for about 5 seconds, until the mixture is a rough puree. Spread the mixture lightly over the center of each tart, leaving a ½-inch border uncovered. Arrange the tomato slices in slightly overlapping concentric circles on top of the prosciutto mixture, starting from the outside edge and working inward. Drizzle a few drops of olive oil over the tomatoes on each tart, then sprinkle on the fresh thyme. Turn up the edges of each tart, making a small ¼-inch border all around. Bake in the center of the oven for 15 to 18 minutes, until the pastry is golden brown.

Remove tarts from the oven and set on a wire rack. Mix the chopped basil with the remaining olive oil and drizzle evenly over all the tarts. Serve immediately. SERVES 6

Tarte aux tomates
Château Saint-Martin

TOMATO AND CHEESE TART PROVENÇAL

For the Herbed Olive Oil

- 1/2 CUP EXTRA-VIRGIN OLIVE OIL
- 1 GARLIC CLOVE, CRUSHED
- 1 BOUQUET GARNI (1 BRANCH OR TEASPOON EACH OF FRESH THYME, ROSEMARY, FENNEL, AND 1 BAY LEAF, TIED WITH THIN STRING OR WRAPPED IN CHEESECLOTH)
- 1/2 TEASPOON SALT
- 1/2 TEASPOON FRESHLY GROUND BLACK PEPPER

For the Tart

- 1 RECIPE PÂTE BRISÉE (PAGE 16), SUBSTITUTING 2 TABLESPOONS EXTRA-VIRGIN OLIVE OIL FOR 2 TABLESPOONS BUTTER, UNBAKED
- 2 TABLESPOONS DIJON MUSTARD
- 2 OUNCES EMMENTAL OR GRUYÈRE CHEESE, GRATED (ABOUT 3/4 CUP)
- 6 MEDIUM TOMATOES, VERY THINLY SLICED
- 1/2 POUND FRESH WHOLE-MILK MOZZARELLA, VERY THINLY SLICED
- 1 TEASPOON FRESH THYME

The aromas of this rustic tart—flavored with thyme, rosemary, fennel, garlic, and rich olive oil—are redolent of the Côte d'Azur back country, where the Château du Domaine St.-Martin, a luxurious, rambling Provençal inn, perches above the town of Vence. Chef Dominique Ferrière creates his tangy tomato tart, popular as an appetizer or as a casual weekend lunch accompanied by a mixed-greens salad, from tomatoes and herbs grown in the Domaine's gardens, and from the fragrant olive oil pressed from the fruit of the property's old olive trees.

Notes: Prepare the herbed oil at least a day in advance. If available, use mozzarella sold in small balls at Italian delicatessens.

To make the herbed oil: In a small glass jar or ceramic bowl, combine the olive oil with the garlic, *bouquet garni*, salt, and pepper. Cover snugly and let marinate at least overnight, or even several days.

Preheat the oven to 375°F.

To make the tart: On a floured work surface, roll out a circle of dough 13 inches across and ⅛-inch thick. Transfer it to a greased 10½-inch black steel tart pan, leaving a ½-inch border extending above the rim. Fold this in half, and press gently all around to smooth. Spread the mustard over the bottom of the shell. Sprinkle the grated cheese over the mustard. Starting at the outside edge of the tart, arrange the tomatoes and mozzarella in alternating, overlapping circles—1 slice of tomato, followed by 1 slice of mozzarella, and so on—working into the center. Sprinkle with the thyme, then drizzle on 2 tablespoons of the herbed olive oil. Bake on the center rack of the oven for 35 to 40 minutes, or until the crust is browned and the cheese is melted and bubbly. Remove from the oven, drizzle on another tablespoon of herbed olive oil (save the remainder for another use), cut into slices, and serve immediately. SERVES 6 TO 8

Tarte aux aubergines de la comtesse Lisa

EGGPLANT–CHÈVRE TART

For the Dough

- 1 TABLESPOON ACTIVE DRY YEAST
- 2/3 CUP LUKEWARM WATER
- 1 3/4 CUPS ALL-PURPOSE FLOUR
- 1 TEASPOON SALT
- 1 TABLESPOON OLIVE OIL

For the Filling

- 4 TABLESPOONS OLIVE OIL
- 1 LARGE GARLIC CLOVE, CRUSHED AND MINCED
- 3 SMALL-TO-MEDIUM EGGPLANTS, CUT INTO SMALL (1/2-INCH) CUBES
- 3 MEDIUM TOMATOES, PEELED, SEEDED, AND MASHED TO A PULP
- 10 OUNCES CREAMY MONTRACHET-STYLE CHÈVRE
- 1/2 CUP PINE NUTS
- 1 TEASPOON FRESH THYME
- 1 TEASPOON SALT
- 1/2 TEASPOON FRESHLY GROUND BLACK PEPPER

Just west of Chartres, behind high wrought-iron gates, lies the handsome and distinguished Château de Blanville, an aristocratic bed-and-breakfast that has been in the family of the young owner, Comte Emmanuel de Cossé-Brissac, for more than 200 years. Emmanuel's wife, the Comtesse Lisa, is a Cordon Bleu–trained chef and former caterer whose imaginative fare, created with many homegrown products from the Blanville gardens, as well as from Chartres' vast open market, makes dinners in the candlelit eighteenth-century dining room truly memorable. This eggplant tart, with chèvre, tomatoes, and pine nuts, is popular for rustic weekend lunches at Blanville.

To make the dough: Combine the yeast and water in a small bowl, stirring to blend. Set aside for 5 minutes. Combine the flour, salt, and olive oil in a food processor or mixing bowl. Process for 5 seconds, or mix, until ingredients resemble soft crumbs. Pour the yeast mixture into the flour and pulse 8 to 10 times, or work together with your fingers, until the dough comes together but before it forms into a firm ball.

Turn the dough out onto a floured work surface and, working with lightly floured hands, knead the dough until all stickiness disappears, about 3 minutes. Form the dough into a soft ball, set into a clean bowl, cover with greased plastic wrap to prevent sticking, and let rise about 1 hour.

On a lightly floured work surface, punch down the dough, then roll it out to a thickness of ¼ inch; you can make this tart in the shape of a rectangle, about 12 x 14 inches, or in a 12- or 13-inch circle. Sprinkle flour or cornmeal over the bottom of a baking sheet. Transfer the dough to the baking sheet, and set aside.

Preheat the oven to 425°F.

To make the filling: In a skillet, heat 3 tablespoons of the olive oil over medium heat. Add the garlic, stir with a wooden spoon, then add the eggplant and mix to coat well with the oil. Cook, stirring frequently, until the eggplant softens and takes on a light golden hue, about 10 minutes. Remove from heat and let cool 5 minutes.

With a pastry brush, apply a 1-inch border of olive oil all around the outside edge of the dough. Spread the tomatoes over the dough, leaving the 1-inch border uncovered. Spread the eggplant mixture on top of the tomatoes. Crumble the chèvre evenly over the top of the tart, scatter the pine nuts evenly, then sprinkle on the thyme, salt, and pepper. Bake in the center of the oven for 20 minutes, or until the crust is browned and the cheese has softened. Serve immediately. Serves 6 to 8

Tarte aux courgettes, coulis de tomates

ZUCCHINI AND BASIL TART WITH FRESH TOMATO SAUCE

For the Tart

- 1 10 1/2-INCH PÂTE SABLÉE SHELL
  (PAGE 18), PARTIALLY BAKED
- 3 TABLESPOONS OLIVE OIL
- 2 POUNDS ZUCCHINI (ABOUT 4 SLIM, 6-INCH
  ZUCCHINI), SLICED INTO 1/8-INCH ROUNDS
- 1/4 CUP FRESH BASIL, FINELY CHOPPED
- 1 TEASPOON SALT
- 1/2 TEASPOON FRESHLY GROUND
  BLACK PEPPER
- 4 LARGE EGGS, BEATEN

For the Tomato Sauce

- 6 SMALL, RIPE BUT FIRM TOMATOES, PEELED,
  SEEDED, AND CHOPPED
- 1 TEASPOON FINES HERBES, FRESH OR DRIED
- 1 GARLIC CLOVE
- 1/2 TEASPOON SALT
- 1/4 TEASPOON FRESH GROUND BLACK PEPPER

This tart smells like a summer morning in the *potager*, or vegetable garden, of the Château des Briottières, the lovely and welcoming family château of François and Hedwige de Valbray in the Anjou region of France, northwest of the Loire Valley. Several years ago François and Hedwige opened their eighteenth-century home surrounded by farm-land to paying guests, who roam the vast property at their leisure, sleep in comfortable bedrooms furnished with family heirlooms, and feast at the big dining room table on savory fare prepared by Hedwige from old family recipes. Her Zucchini and Basil Tart, accompanied by a cold fresh tomato sauce, is a summertime favorite of her guests.

Preheat the oven to 375°F.

To make the tart: Heat the olive oil in a large frying pan. Add the zucchini and stir them until they are well coated with the oil. Lower the heat slightly and cook the zucchini until they begin to turn translucent; do not let them brown. Remove from the heat and drain the oil and liquid from the zucchini in a colander.

Arrange the zucchini in the baked crust, spreading them evenly over the bottom. Add the basil, salt, and pepper to the beaten eggs, and mix with a whisk until blended. Pour the egg mixture over the zucchini and bake the tart in the center of the oven for about 40 minutes, until the crust is a deep golden brown and the filling is firm and browned in parts. Cool on a wire rack for 15 minutes.

To make the sauce: Combine all the ingredients in a food processor or blender and mix until pureed. Chill until ready to serve.

Serve the warm tart with the cold tomato sauce. SERVES 6

Tarte provençale à la courge

PROVENÇAL SQUASH TART

For the Pastry
- 1 1/2 CUPS ALL-PURPOSE FLOUR
- 8 TABLESPOONS OLIVE OIL
- 4 TABLESPOONS COLD WATER
- 1 TEASPOON SALT

For the Filling
- 6 TABLESPOONS OLIVE OIL
- 1 POUND (4 MEDIUM) ONIONS, VERY FINELY CHOPPED
- 2 BAY LEAVES
- 2 SPRIGS FRESH OR DRIED THYME
- 3 POUNDS (APPROXIMATELY 1 MEDIUM) WINTER OR ACORN SQUASH, PEELED AND DICED VERY SMALL
- 4 LARGE EGGS, LIGHTLY BEATEN
- 2 1/2 CUPS GRUYÈRE CHEESE, FRESHLY GRATED (ABOUT 6 OUNCES)
- 1 CUP COOKED LONG-GRAIN RICE
- 1 TEASPOON SALT
- 1/4 TEASPOON FRESHLY GROUND BLACK PEPPER
- 1/2 CUP UNSEASONED BREAD CRUMBS

High on a hill in lower Provence, just a short drive from the Mediterranean harbor towns of Bandol and Sanary-sur-Mer, sits a lovely village inn called the Hostellerie Bérard. The inn, the creation of renowned local chef René Bérard and his dynamic wife, Danièle, dominates the main street of La Cadière d'Azur, an old-fashioned Provençal village that might have sprung full-blown from the novels of Marcel Pagnol. Sweet breezes scented with thyme and lavender waft through the luminous yellow dining room where René's savory creations, such as this scrumptious squash tart, tempt diners from throughout Provence and the Riviera up the steep, winding road to La Cadière.

To make the pastry: In the bowl of a food processor, combine the flour, olive oil, water, and salt. Process about 12 seconds until ingredients are well-blended and crumbly. Remove from the bowl, knead in your hands for 2 minutes—adding a bit of flour if the dough seems too oily—then press into a disk, wrap in plastic wrap, and refrigerate for 1 hour.

On a floured work surface, roll out the dough to a circle 14 inches in diameter and ⅛-inch thick. Transfer the dough to a greased 10½-inch tart pan, pressing the dough gently into the corners and sides of the pan. Trim the edges, leaving a ⅓-inch border extending above the pan. Fold this ⅓ inch of dough over upon itself and pinch the edges gently all around, or crimp lightly with a fork to make a design. Prick the bottom all over with a fork. Cover with plastic wrap and refrigerate for 20 minutes.

Preheat the oven to 375°F.

Line the tart shell with aluminum foil, then fill with rice or dried beans. Bake for 20 minutes. Remove rice or beans and aluminum foil, bake 2 more minutes, then set aside on a wire rack to cool.

To make the filling: Warm 3 tablespoons of the olive oil in a large skillet over medium heat. Add the onions, bay leaves, and thyme, lower the heat to medium low, and cook slowly, stirring occasionally to prevent browning, until the onions are translucent and just beginning to get tinged with gold, about 25 minutes. Remove the bay leaves and thyme, add the squash, drizzle in the remaining olive oil, and stir well to combine with the onions. Cook slowly, stirring occasionally, until the squash "melts" into a soft mush, about 40 minutes. Transfer the mixture into a bowl, let cool, cover with plastic wrap, and refrigerate 1 hour.

Preheat the oven to 375°F.

Mash and stir the squash mixture to remove any remaining lumps. Add the eggs and cheese and whisk briskly to blend. Then add the rice, salt, and pepper and stir with a wooden spoon to combine. Pour into the tart shell, sprinkle the bread crumbs over the top, and bake on the center rack of the oven for 35 to 40 minutes, until the top is browned and the filling is firm in the center. Set on a wire rack for 10 minutes. Serve warm, accompanied by a crisp green salad of mesclun or arugula and a chilled rosé wine from Provence. SERVES 6 TO 8

Note: The filling for this tart also makes a delicious side dish for turkey, roast pork, or grilled swordfish. Prepare the filling as directed, pour into a buttered ceramic casserole or other oven-to-table baking dish, top with bread crumbs, and bake at 350°F for 30 minutes.

Gâteau de pommes boulangère

BAKER'S WIFE POTATO AND CHÈVRE PIE

- 1 RECIPE PÂTE FEUILLETÉE RAPIDE (PAGE 21), OR 2 SHEETS COMMERCIAL PUFF PASTRY, CHILLED BUT NOT FROZEN

- 1 CUP MILK

- 8 OUNCES CREAMY MONTRACHET-STYLE CHÈVRE

- 2 LARGE EGGS, LIGHTLY BEATEN

- 1/2 CUP (4 OUNCES) CRÈME FRAÎCHE OR HEAVY CREAM

- 1/2 CUP ALL-PURPOSE FLOUR

- 1 TEASPOON SALT

- 1/4 TEASPOON FRESHLY GROUND BLACK PEPPER

- 1/4 TEASPOON GROUND NUTMEG

- 1 1/2 POUNDS YUKON GOLD, WHITE ROSE, OR CREAMER POTATOES, PARBOILED FOR 10 MINUTES, PEELED, AND CUT INTO 1/8-INCH SLICES

- 1 EGG, LIGHTLY BEATEN, FOR GLAZE

This delicious covered tart, with its golden, flaky crust, is a variation of the classic French potato dish *pommes boulangère*, or "baker's wife potatoes," a mixture of potatoes and cheese baked in the always-hot baker's oven by the baker's wife before dinner. Jean-Luc Poujauran, a top Paris baker with a charming turn-of-the-century shop near the Eiffel Tower, developed this recipe to serve to friends on a casual Sunday evening at home, accompanied by a hearty red wine and a big green salad.

Divide the dough in half and roll out each half into a rough circle about 13 inches in diameter and ⅛ inch thick. (If you're working with rectangular sheets of commercial pastry, trim a couple of inches off each of the shorter ends and press them onto the bottom edge of the dough to create a 12-inch square.) Trim each piece of dough into a neat 12-inch circle, using a plate or a large pot cover as a guide. Brush the bottom and sides of a 10- or 11-inch tart pan, or slope-sided ovenproof skillet, with a pastry brush dampened with water. Press 1 circle of pastry crust into the bottom and up the sides of the tart pan or skillet. Cover with plastic wrap, wrap the remaining circle of dough in plastic wrap, and refrigerate all pastry.

Preheat the oven to 400°F.

In a large, heavy saucepan, combine the milk and cheese. Over medium heat, stir the mixture constantly until it is hot but not boiling and all the cheese has melted. Remove from the heat and set aside.

Combine the eggs with the *crème fraîche* in a medium, heavy saucepan. Over medium heat, stir to blend. Add the flour, salt, pepper, and nutmeg, stirring constantly to keep the bottom from burning. After a minute or two, when the mixture has thickened, remove from the heat and pour into the cheese mixture, mixing well with a wooden spoon to blend.

Remove the pastry crust in the pan from the refrigerator. Spread a third of the cheese mixture over the bottom of the crust. Arrange half the potato slices in slightly overlapping concentric circles on top of the cheese layer, working inward from the outside edge. Spread a second third of the cheese mixture over the potato layer. Layer the remaining half of the potatoes over the cheese, and, finally, spread the last third of the cheese mixture over the top of the potatoes. Remove the other circle of dough from the refrigerator and lay it on top of the potato and cheese filling. Seal the 2 halves of pastry crust around the inside edge of the pan, rather than around the top of the pan as with a standard pie or covered tart. Pinch the dough together with your fingertips, making sure it is well

sealed, or join the 2 halves by using a butter knife and pressing the dough between your finger and the knife, into a vertical "ridge" pattern.

Brush the top of the pie with the egg glaze, then score the dough with 2 small cross-hatch (#) designs and make a ½-inch vent in the top of the crust—Jean-Luc calls it a *cheminée* (chimney)—to let the steam out as it bakes. Set the pie in the center of the oven and cook for 30 minutes. Reduce the heat to 350°F and bake another 30 minutes, until the crust is a rich golden brown. (If the crust starts to get too dark after 45 minutes or so, cover lightly with a sheet of aluminum foil and continue baking until the end of the cooking time.) Cool on a wire rack for 20 minutes before serving. SERVES 6

Note: This tart is delicious as a main course accompanied by a simple salad of mixed greens, such as mesclun, dressed with a shallot vinaigrette. (To make this simple vinaigrette, combine 1 minced small shallot, ¼ teaspoon salt, and ¼ teaspoon freshly ground black pepper in a bowl. Add 1 tablespoon red wine vinegar (preferably French, with a 7 percent acidity) and 4 tablespoons olive oil. Let sit for 30 minutes, then blend well with a fork or whisk and pour over the greens; toss 1 minute before serving.)

Quiche aux escargots, choucroute et pommes de terre

SNAIL, SAUERKRAUT, AND POTATO QUICHE

- 1 PÂTE BRISÉE SHELL (PAGE 16), UNBAKED

- 2 DOZEN SMALL ESCARGOTS

- 1 CUP RIESLING OR OTHER DRY, FRUITY WHITE WINE

- 1/2 POUND SMALL BAKING POTATOES, SUCH AS RUSSETS, PEELED AND VERY THINLY SLICED

- SALT AND FRESHLY GROUND BLACK PEPPER TO TASTE

- 1/2 POUND SAUERKRAUT

- 1 CUP GRUYÈRE CHEESE, FRESHLY GRATED (ABOUT 3 OUNCES)

- 1 CUP HEAVY CREAM

- 1/3 CUP MILK

- 6 LARGE EGG YOLKS

- 1 TEASPOON SALT

- 1/8 TEASPOON GROUND NUTMEG

- 1/2 CUP CHIVES, CUT INTO 1/2-INCH PIECES

- 1/4 POUND SLAB BACON, CHOPPED INTO SMALL PIECES AND LIGHTLY BROWNED

From the imagination of Michel Husser, the creative two-star chef at his family's Hostellerie du Cerf in Marlenheim in northern Alsace, comes this unusual but felicitous combination of diverse elements. *Choucroute*—sauerkraut—snails, and potatoes are all basic ingredients in Alsatian cuisine, so it is not a complete surprise to find them assembled together in a quiche, a classic Alsatian specialty. The combination is a delicious one that will surprise your guests. If you are not a snail lover (and I confess I am not), you can substitute slices of weisswurst or bockwurst (mild white veal sausages) for the snails, or simply make the tart without them.

Preheat the oven to 375°F.

Place the *escargots* in a strainer and rinse well under cold water. Transfer to a small saucepan and add the wine. Bring to a boil over medium-high heat, then reduce to medium low and simmer 5 minutes. Remove from the heat and let cool.

Arrange the potato slices in the bottom of the tart shell. Season lightly with salt and pepper. Rinse the sauerkraut well through a colander, once with hot water and twice with cold water. Press out excess water using the back of a fork and pat dry with paper towels. Chop the sauerkraut into coleslaw-size pieces, sprinkle with salt and pepper, then toss with the cheese in a mixing bowl. Drain the *escargots* and arrange them evenly on top of the potatoes, then cover with the sauerkraut-cheese mixture.

In a mixing bowl, combine the cream, milk, egg yolks, salt, and nutmeg and whisk briskly until well blended. Stir in the chives. Pour the cream mixture into the tart shell, then scatter the bacon evenly over the top. Bake in the center of the oven for 45 to 50 minutes, until the crust is well browned and the center of the tart is set. Cool on a wire rack for 5 minutes, then serve hot. SERVES 6 TO 8

Tarte chaude de maquereau à la pipérade

WARM PIPÉRADE-MACKEREL TART

For the Tart

- 1 RECIPE PÂTE BRISÉE À L'OEUF (PAGE 17), UNBAKED
- 3 TABLESPOONS OLIVE OIL
- 2 SMALL ONIONS, FINELY CHOPPED
- 2 GARLIC CLOVES, FINELY CHOPPED
- 2 SMALL GREEN PEPPERS, SEEDED AND FINELY CHOPPED
- 1 LARGE RED BELL PEPPER, SEEDED AND FINELY CHOPPED
- 1 SPRIG FRESH OR DRIED THYME
- 4 SMALL TOMATOES, SEEDED, CORED, AND FINELY CHOPPED
- 1 TEASPOON SALT
- 1/4 TEASPOON FRESHLY GROUND BLACK PEPPER
- 1 POUND SPANISH MACKEREL, SLICED IN SASHIMI-LIKE STRIPS, 5 X 1 X 1/4-INCHES

For the Vinaigrette

- 1/4 CUP OLIVE OIL
- 2 TABLESPOONS BALSAMIC VINEGAR
- 1/2 TEASPOON SALT
- 1/2 TEASPOON COARSELY GROUND BLACK PEPPER
- 1/2 CUP CHIVES, SLICED IN 1-INCH LENGTHS

One of my favorite Paris hotels is the elegant Hôtel Le Parc in the sixteenth *arrondissement*, not far from the Trocadéro. Created from five turn-of-the-century townhouses surrounding a cobbled courtyard-garden, Le Parc has lovely rooms with an English country decor and a sleek, contemporary bistro—Le Relais du Parc—that draws fashionable neighborhood diners with its upscale bistro fare. One of the imaginative starters often on the menu is this made-to-order individual tart that layers pizza-like disks of *pâte brisée*, a *pipérade* filling, and a topping of thin Spanish mackerel fillets drizzled with a balsamic vinaigrette. Only the mild, delicately flavored Spanish mackerel will do here; Boston mackerel is too strong and oily.

To make the tart: Heat the olive oil in a large skillet over medium heat. Add the onions and garlic and cook until they are slightly translucent but not browned, about 5 minutes. Add the green and red peppers and the thyme, and mix in with a wooden spoon. Stir in the tomatoes, salt, and pepper, and reduce heat to medium low. Cook the vegetable mixture slowly, stirring occasionally to prevent browning, until the moisture evaporates, about 30 minutes. Let cool, transfer to a bowl, and set aside.

Preheat the oven to 375°F.

Roll out the dough to a thickness of ⅛ inch. Using a pot cover or an inverted cereal bowl as a guide, cut out four 5-inch circles. Transfer them to a lightly greased baking sheet, prick each several times with a fork, then bake on the center rack of the oven for about 15 minutes, until they are lightly browned. Transfer to a wire rack to cool.

Preheat the broiler.

Return the pastry circles to a baking sheet. Spread each equally with the *pipérade*. Top the *pipérade* with the thin slices of mackerel. Season with salt and pepper, then set under the broiler for 2 to 3 minutes, just until the mackerel fillets turn white.

To make the vinaigrette: Combine the oil and vinegar in a bowl, but do not emulsify. Season with salt and pepper. Drizzle the vinaigrette over the top of the tarts, then sprinkle on the chives. Serve immediately.

SERVES 4

Tourte à la morue et aux pommes de terre

ANDRÉ SOLTNER'S SALTED CODFISH AND POTATO TART

- 1 9-INCH PÂTE FEUILLETÉE RAPIDE SHELL (PAGE 21), UNBAKED, PLUS 1 10-INCH CIRCLE OF DOUGH TO COVER, OR 4 SHEETS COMMERCIAL PUFF PASTRY, CHILLED BUT NOT FROZEN
- 12 OUNCES SALTED CODFISH
- 1 1/4 POUNDS RUSSET OR IDAHO POTATOES, PEELED AND CUT INTO 1/8-INCH SLICES
- 1/4 CUP CHOPPED PARSLEY
- 1 TEASPOON SALT
- 1/4 TEASPOON FRESHLY GROUND BLACK PEPPER
- 5 LARGE EGGS, HARD-BOILED, PEELED, AND THINLY SLICED
- 1/2 CUP CRÈME FRAÎCHE OR HEAVY CREAM
- 1 LARGE EGG, BEATEN WITH 1 TABLESPOON WATER, FOR GLAZE

Long-time habitués of New York's celebrated restaurant Lutèce fondly remember the hearty Alsatian main-course tarts that former chef-owner André Soltner would occasionally prepare for regulars he knew would appreciate them. One favorite was a tart composed of potatoes, eggs, bacon, and *crème fraîche* that Mr. Soltner remembers his mother making for him as a child in his native Thann, a town in Alsace. On a recent Sunday, when friends were visiting the weekend home he shares with his wife, Simone, in upstate New York, Mr. Soltner created an interesting variation of this classic tart, substituting salted codfish for the bacon. Served with a crisp green salad and a chilled, fragrant Pinot Gris from Alsace, it's a delight.

Note: The salted codfish must be soaked at least 24 hours before preparing the tart.

Soak the fish in a large pot of cold water for 24 hours, making sure the water completely covers the fish. Change the water 3 times during the 24-hour period. Cut the codfish into several large pieces, then place them in a pot of lightly salted water. Bring to a boil and simmer for 10 minutes. Remove the fish from the water and pat dry. Remove any remaining skin and bones from the fish, then flake into small pieces.

Rinse the potato slices in cold water to remove any starch, drain, and pat dry. Toss the potatoes with the parsley, salt, and pepper. Arrange half the potatoes in an overlapping layer in the bottom of the tart shell. Cover with the flaked codfish, followed by a layer of the egg slices. Top with an over-lapping layer of the remaining potatoes. Spread the *crème fraîche* evenly over the potatoes. Brush the edges of the lower crust with some of the egg glaze, then cover the tart with the circle of pastry dough. Trim the edge to fit, then crimp together with a fork to seal well. Prick the top in several places with the tip of a sharp knife. Chill in the refrigerator.

Preheat the oven to 400°F.

Brush the top crust lightly with the remaining egg glaze. Bake the tart for 20 minutes on the middle shelf of the oven, then lower the temperature to 350°F and bake 1 hour longer. Lower the oven temperature to 300°F and bake 10 minutes more, until the crust is a deep golden brown. Let cool on a wire rack for 10 minutes, then serve warm. SERVES 6

Tarte méditerranée au thon frais

MEDITERRANEAN TUNA TART

- 1 9-INCH PÂTE BRISÉE À L'OEUF SHELL (PAGE 17), SUBSTITUTING 2 TABLESPOONS OLIVE OIL FOR 2 TABLESPOONS BUTTER IN RECIPE, FULLY BAKED

- 3 6-OUNCE CANS WHITE ALBACORE TUNA, PACKED IN OIL

- 1/2 CUP PLUS 3 TABLESPOONS EXTRA-VIRGIN OLIVE OIL

- 1 LARGE PEARL ONION, THINLY SLICED

- 6 LARGE SHALLOTS, THINLY SLICED

- 1 LARGE GARLIC CLOVE, FINELY CHOPPED

- 1 SPRIG FRESH OR DRIED THYME

- 2 BAY LEAVES

- 1 TEASPOON SALT

- 1/2 TEASPOON FRESHLY GROUND BLACK PEPPER

- 3/4 CUP CHOPPED FRESH CHIVES

- 3/4 CUP CHOPPED FRESH CORIANDER

- 4 LARGE BASIL LEAVES, FINELY CHOPPED

- 2 LARGE BASIL LEAVES FOR GARNISH

- 10 NIÇOISE OLIVES

Surrounded on three sides by the azure sea and bathed by the bright white sun, La Réserve de Beaulieu, a lavish and lovely resort hotel on the Riviera, is the perfect setting to nibble on Chef Guillaume Sourrieu's intensely flavored Mediterranean Tuna Tart. Rich and aromatic, with shallots, chives, thyme, basil, fresh coriander, and garlic enhancing the tuna, this easy-to-prepare tart makes a distinctive hors d'oeuvre when cut in narrow wedges and accompanied by an apéritif, or a flavorful appetizer when served with a mesclun salad.

Heat 3 tablespoons of olive oil in a large skillet over medium heat. Add the onion, shallots, garlic, thyme, bay leaves, salt, and pepper. Stir with a wooden or plastic spatula to combine with the oil, then reduce heat to medium low and cook just until the onions and shallots become translucent, about 4 minutes. Do not let them brown. Remove from the heat, pick out the bay leaves and thyme, and set aside to cool.

Drain the tuna. In the bowl of an electric mixer, flake the tuna with a fork. Add the onion mixture, the chives, the coriander, and the basil. Mix on medium-low speed and slowly drizzle in all but 1 tablespoon of olive oil. Mix, scraping down the sides of the bowl, until well blended, about 1 minute. Spread the mixture over the bottom of the tart shell.

Warm the remaining tablespoon of olive oil in a small pan. Remove from heat, then coat the basil leaves with the oil and arrange in the center of the tart. Scatter the olives evenly over the top of the tart, cut into wedges, and serve at room temperature or slightly chilled. SERVES 6 AS AN APPETIZER

Tartelettes Napoléon au Saumon fumé

NAPOLEON-STYLE SMOKED SALMON TARTLETS

For the Filling

- 12 SLICES SMOKED SALMON, AT LEAST 3 INCHES WIDE (ABOUT 3/4 POUND)
- 1 CUP CRÈME FRAÎCHE
- 3 TABLESPOONS DILL, FINELY CHOPPED
- 1 TABLESPOON MINCED SHALLOT
- SALT AND FRESHLY GROUND BLACK PEPPER
- 1 TEASPOON LEMON JUICE

For the Vinaigrette

- 6 MEDIUM OYSTERS, REMOVED FROM SHELLS, RESERVED WITH THEIR LIQUOR
- 1/4 CUP OLIVE OIL
- 1/4 CUP GRAPESEED, ALMOND KERNEL, OR SUNFLOWER OIL
- JUICE OF 1/2 LEMON

For the Pastry

- 1/2 CUP ALL-PURPOSE FLOUR
- 3 LARGE EGG WHITES
- 3 TABLESPOONS LUKEWARM CLARIFIED UNSALTED BUTTER
- 1/2 CUP CLAM JUICE

Bernard Loiseau puts a personal spin on every dish served at his romantic three-star restaurant, La Côte d'Or, in the Burgundian village of Saulieu. Flavors are intense and true, and components of a dish are woven together with a masterly interplay of texture. In this heavenly appetizer, Chef Loiseau's extremely broad interpretation of the tart, crisp paper-thin pastry disks—savory first cousins to the tile cookie—are stacked three tall and filled with smoked salmon and a dill-and-shallot-studded salmon cream. The *coup de maître* of this mouthwatering creation is the sensuous, creamy oyster vinaigrette that surrounds the tartlet: its briny, sea-rich flavors complement and heighten the subtle, smoky taste of the salmon.

Note: The filling and the vinaigrette can be prepared several hours in advance. The pastry is best prepared shortly before serving.

To make the filling: Using a ramequin or a cookie cutter as a guide, cut out a 3-inch circle from each salmon slice. Transfer to a dish, cover with plastic wrap, and refrigerate.

In a mixing bowl, whisk the *crème fraîche* until it has the fluffy consistency of thick whipped cream. (Do not overbeat or it will quickly turn into butter!) Chop the remaining pieces of salmon into little bits and, using a rubber or wooden spatula, slowly incorporate them into the whipped cream. Add 2 tablespoons dill, the shallot, a pinch of salt and pepper, and the teaspoon of lemon juice, and carefully blend them into the salmon cream, maintaining as much volume as possible. Cover with plastic wrap and refrigerate.

To make the vinaigrette: Combine the oysters, half their liquor, the oils, and the lemon juice in a blender or small bowl of a food processor. Emulsify until the mixture is thick and creamy. Transfer to a small bowl, stir in a pinch of freshly ground black pepper, cover with plastic wrap, and refrigerate.

To make the pastry: Sift the flour into a mixing bowl, then make a well in the center. Pour the egg whites into the well and whisk briskly until the ingredients are combined in a satiny batter. Slowly pour in the clarified butter and clam juice, and whisk briskly until the batter is thick and creamy. Cover with plastic wrap and refrigerate at least 2 hours.

Preheat the oven to 400°F.

On a nonstick baking sheet, place tablespoonsful of the pastry batter 6 inches apart. Using the back of a fork, gently spread the batter into almost translucent 3-inch circles. Bake in the center of the oven for about 7 minutes, just until the edges start to turn brown. Transfer to a wire rack with a spatula to cool and crisp.

Assemble the tartlets just before serving. In the center of each serving plate, place a pastry tile. Cover it with a slice of salmon and a tablespoon of salmon cream. Cover this with the second tile, another slice of salmon, and the cream. Finish with the third tile, salmon, and finally a small mound of the salmon cream. Spoon the oyster vinaigrette around the tartlets, garnish with the remaining tablespoon of chopped dill, and serve immediately. SERVES 4

Wine note: An elegant white Burgundy from the Côte d'Or, such as a Meursault, a Puligny-Montrachet, or a top California Chardonnay, would be the ideal accompaniment for this sophisticated appetizer.

Tarte au Saumon et aux endives

CHÂTEAU LAMOTHE'S SALMON-ENDIVE TART

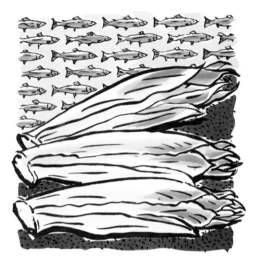

- 1 10 1/2-INCH PÂTE FEUILLETÉE RAPIDE SHELL (PAGE 21), PARTIALLY BAKED, OR 4 SHEETS COMMERCIAL PUFF PASTRY TO LINE A 10 1/2-INCH BUTTERED TART PAN, PARTIALLY BAKED AS DIRECTED

- 2 TABLESPOONS UNSALTED BUTTER

- 3 MEDIUM ENDIVE, WASHED AND CUT LENGTHWISE INTO JULIENNE STRIPS

- 1/2 POUND SMOKED SALMON, CUT INTO SMALL PIECES

- 4 LARGE EGGS

- 1/2 CUP CRÈME FRAÎCHE AND 1/4 CUP MILK, OR 3/4 CUP HEAVY CREAM

- 2 TABLESPOONS FRESH DILL, CHOPPED

- 1/4 TEASPOON FRESHLY GROUND BLACK PEPPER

During the hectic days of VinExpo, Bordeaux's mammoth international wine festival held every two years in June, one of the most sought-after invitations is to a candlelight dinner on the terrace of Château Lamothe in Haux. *Châtelains* Anne and Fabrice Néel, producers of an excellent line of both red and white wines, preside over these convivial events, where the cuisine is always memorable and the *joie de vivre* contagious. Anne and her mother, Madame Perriquet, spend days in the kitchen preparing feasts for the international *invités* who crowd their tables. The Tarte au Saumon et aux Endives is a succulent appetizer tart that Lamothe guests enjoy as a first course accompanied by a glass or two of crisp, chilled Sauvignon Blanc straight from the cellars.

Preheat the oven to 375°F.

Heat the butter in a large skillet over medium-low heat. Add the endive, stir to coat them with the butter, and cook for about 10 minutes, stirring frequently, until they are lightly browned and translucent. Spread the endive over the bottom of the tart shell, then spread the salmon on top of the endive.

In a large bowl, combine the eggs, *crème fraîche* and milk or the heavy cream, dill, and pepper. Whisk the mixture until well blended, then pour into the tart shell. Bake in the center of the oven for 35 to 40 minutes, until the crust is browned and the center of the tart is firm. Cool slightly on a wire rack. Serve warm. SERVES 6 TO 8

Tarte au saumon et à l'oseille

SMOKED SALMON-SORREL TART

- 1 10 1/2-INCH PÂTE BRISÉE SHELL (PAGE 16), PARTIALLY BAKED

- 1/2 POUND SORREL, WASHED AND STEMS TRIMMED

- 6 LARGE EGGS

- 1 CUP CRÈME FRAÎCHE

- 1/2 CUP HEAVY CREAM

- 1/2 TEASPOON GROUND WHITE PEPPER

- 1/2 POUND SMOKED SALMON, CUT INTO THIN JULIENNE STRIPS ABOUT 1 1/2 INCHES LONG

Displayed on a marble-topped sideboard in a corner of Les Nuits des Thés, a sophisticated Left Bank Paris tearoom set among the galleries and antique shops of the rue de Beaune, this appealing smoked salmon tart catches the eye, and the fancy, of many a lady who lunches here. The subtle sourness of the sorrel and the *crème fraîche* is a pleasing counterpoint to the rich smokiness of the salmon.

Preheat the oven to 400°F.

Reserve 6 sorrel leaves for the garnish. Drop the remaining sorrel into a pot of boiling water, reduce to a simmer, and cook for 5 minutes. Drain well, pressing out excess water, then puree several seconds in a food processor or blender.

In a medium mixing bowl, combine the eggs, *crème fraîche*, cream, and pepper. Beat with a whisk until well blended. Add the sorrel puree and the smoked salmon, and gently whisk to combine. Pour the salmon filling into the tart shell. If you wish, decorate the top with the reserved sorrel leaves, cut and arranged at whim. Bake in the center of the oven for 30 minutes, until the crust is golden brown and the center of the tart is set. Remove to a wire rack to cool. Serve lukewarm or at room temperature. SERVES 6 TO 8

Tarte aux poireaux

LEEK TART

- 1 10 1/2-INCH PÂTE BRISÉE SHELL (PAGE 16), UNBAKED
- 2 POUNDS YOUNG, SLIM, AND SMALL LEEKS
- 3 TABLESPOONS UNSALTED BUTTER
- 3 TABLESPOONS OLIVE OIL
- 2 TABLESPOONS ALL-PURPOSE FLOUR
- 3 LARGE EGGS
- 1/2 CUP CRÈME FRAÎCHE OR HEAVY CREAM
- 1/4 CUP FROMAGE BLANC, OR WHOLE-MILK RICOTTA CHEESE, WHIPPED IN A BLENDER
- 1 1/4 TEASPOONS SALT
- 1/2 TEASPOON GROUND WHITE PEPPER
- 1/4 TEASPOON FRESHLY GROUND BLACK PEPPER
- 1/4 TEASPOON GROUND NUTMEG

The leek tart, offered by many Paris bistros as an appetizer, also makes a fine light supper or an attractive addition to a brunch buffet. This recipe is a favorite at-home dish of Paris baker Jean-Luc Poujauran, who likes to buy his ingredients at the Sunday morning *Marché Biologique*—the open-air organic market—on the rue de Rennes. A crisp, fruity white wine, such as a Riesling or a Chardonnay, is a perfect accompaniment.

Preheat the oven to 400°F.

Trim and discard the root ends and leafy green tops of the leeks, leaving only the white and pale green stalks. Slice the leeks in 1/4-inch rounds, then soak them briefly in cold water to remove all sand and grit. Drain well.

Combine the butter and olive oil in a large skillet. Warm the mixture over low heat until the butter melts. Stir in the leeks, cover the pan, and cook over low heat, stirring occasionally, until the leeks are just tender but not browned, about 15 minutes. Uncover, sprinkle in the flour, and stir well to blend. Remove from the heat and set aside.

In a medium bowl, whisk together the eggs, *crème fraîche*, and *fromage blanc* until smoothly blended. Stir in the salt, peppers, and nutmeg. Add the leeks and mix well. Pour the filling into the prepared pastry shell. Bake in the center of the oven for 35 to 40 minutes, or until the top of the tart is puffed and lightly golden brown. Cool on a wire rack for 15 minutes before serving. SERVES 6

Note: For mail-order sources for a wonderful fat-free *fromage blanc*—a ricotta-like cheese with the consistency of sour cream—see the Appendix on page 123.

Tarte provençale de Cador

CADOR'S PROVENÇAL TART

- 1 10 1/2-INCH PÂTE BRISÉE SHELL (PAGE 16), UNBAKED

- 2 TABLESPOONS UNSALTED BUTTER

- 1 LARGE GREEN PEPPER (ABOUT 1/2 POUND), SEEDED AND CHOPPED

- 2 MEDIUM ONIONS, DICED

- 1 SMALL EGGPLANT (ABOUT 1/2 POUND), CUT INTO 1/2-INCH CUBES

- 2 MEDIUM TOMATOES, PEELED, SEEDED, AND CHOPPED

- 2 1/2 CUPS GRUYÈRE OR SWISS CHEESE, GRATED (ABOUT 1/2 POUND)

- 5 LARGE EGGS

- 1 CUP MILK

- 2/3 CUP CRÈME FRAÎCHE

- 1 TEASPOON SALT

- 1/4 TEASPOON FRESHLY GROUND BLACK PEPPER

Just steps from the Louvre, in the shadow of the lavishly sculpted Gothic church Saint-Germain-l'Auxerrois, the small, old-fashioned tearoom–*pâtisserie* Cador has been serving luscious confections since it opened its doors in 1885. The clientele is virtually unchanged from the end of the nineteenth century, composed today, as it was then, of browsers at the Louvre, shoppers at the nearby Samaritaine department store, and hungry gourmands coming from Sunday morning mass. The Cadors— Sylvie, the sweet-faced hostess, and her *pâtissier* husband, Félicien—have been at the helm since 1966, treating customers to a range of sweet and savory pastries, including this Provençal tart.

Preheat the oven to 400°F.

In a large skillet, melt the butter over medium heat. Add the green pepper, onion, and eggplant and cook until the vegetables begin to soften and the onions begin to look translucent, about 5 minutes. Stir frequently so that the vegetables don't stick or burn. Add the tomatoes and cook until the vegetables are soft and the onions turn very pale golden brown, about 7 to 10 minutes more. Remove from the heat, drain excess liquid from the pan, then spoon the vegetables into the tart shell. Sprinkle the cheese over the vegetables.

In a medium bowl, beat the eggs with a whisk, then add the milk, *crème fraîche*, salt, and pepper. Whisk until blended. Pour the egg mixture over the vegetables, filling the tart to just below the brim of the crust. Set the tart on the center rack of the oven, reduce heat to 375°F, and bake 40 to 45 minutes, until the crust is nicely browned and the center of the tart is firm. Cool for a few minutes on a wire rack, then serve warm. SERVES 6 TO 8

Wine note: This tart is also nicely complemented by a lively Provençal rosé from Bandol, or a classic Tavel rosé, produced near Avignon.

Pichade au maquet

PROVENÇAL ONION–ANCHOVY–BLACK OLIVE TART

For the Dough

- 1 TABLESPOON ACTIVE DRY YEAST
- 2/3 CUP LUKEWARM WATER
- 2 CUPS ALL-PURPOSE FLOUR
- 1 TEASPOON SALT
- 3 TABLESPOONS OLIVE OIL

For the Filling

- 3 TABLESPOONS OLIVE OIL
- 1 POUND (ABOUT 4 MEDIUM) ONIONS, VERY THINLY SLICED
- 1 LARGE SPRIG FRESH THYME
- 2 SMALL BAY LEAVES
- 1/4 TEASPOON SALT
- 1/4 TEASPOON FRESHLY GROUND BLACK PEPPER
- 4 TABLESPOONS ANCHOVY PASTE
- 1/2 CUP OIL-CURED BLACK OLIVES, PITTED AND HALVED
- 10 SMALL GARLIC CLOVES, UNPEELED
- 1/2 CUP LOOSELY PACKED FLAT PARSLEY LEAVES

Also known as *pissaladière*, this version of the classic Provençal tart from René Bérard calls for anchovy paste rather than anchovy fillets to accompany the caramelized onions and black olives atop the crusty dough. I love to make this for hors d'oeuvres, sliced into long, narrow triangles and served with chilled rosé wine.

To make the dough: Combine the yeast and water in a small bowl, stir, then set aside for 5 minutes. In the bowl of an electric mixer, combine the flour with the yeast mixture, salt, and olive oil. Beat until ingredients are thoroughly blended. Remove from the bowl and knead on a floured work surface, adding a bit more flour if the dough is sticky, until the dough is smooth and elastic, 8 to 10 minutes. Transfer the dough to a bowl, cover loosely with plastic wrap, and let rise at room temperature for 1 hour.

To make the filling: Heat the olive oil in a large skillet over medium heat, then add the onions, thyme, bay leaves, salt, and pepper. Reduce the heat to low, then cook the onion mixture slowly until the onions are soft, translucent, and slightly golden—but not browned—about 45 minutes. Remove the bay leaves and thyme and set aside to cool.

Punch down the dough, then roll out on a lightly floured surface to a circle ¼-inch thick. Transfer the dough to a lightly greased baking sheet. Spread the anchovy paste over the bottom of the tart, leaving a ½-inch border. Spread the onion mixture over the anchovy paste. Scatter on the black olives and the garlic cloves. Let stand for 15 minutes.

Preheat the oven to 375°F.

Bake tart in the center of the oven for 15 minutes. Scatter on the parsley leaves and bake for another 15 minutes, until the edges of the tart are nicely browned. Drizzle a bit of olive oil over the tart. Cut into tiny wedges for hors d'oeuvres or larger slices for an appetizer and serve immediately. SERVES 6 FOR APPETIZERS, MORE FOR HORS D'OEUVRES

Tourte Vosgienne

ALSATIAN MEAT TART

For the Tart

- 1 10 1/2-INCH PÂTE FEUILLETÉE RAPIDE SHELL (PAGE 21), UNBAKED, OR 4 SHEETS COMMERCIAL PUFF PASTRY AND 1 11-INCH CIRCLE OF DOUGH TO COVER
- 1 1/2 POUNDS PORK LOIN, CUT INTO VERY THIN JULIENNE STRIPS, ABOUT 1 1/2 INCHES LONG
- 1/4 CUP CURLY PARSLEY, FINELY CHOPPED
- 2 TABLESPOONS MINCED ONION
- 2 TABLESPOONS MINCED SHALLOT
- 1 TEASPOON SALT
- 1/4 TEASPOON FRESHLY GROUND BLACK PEPPER
- 1 TABLESPOON LIGHT OLIVE OR VEGETABLE OIL
- 1/2 CUP RIESLING OR OTHER DRY WHITE WINE
- 1 LARGE EGG, BEATEN WITH 1 TEASPOON WATER, FOR GLAZE

For the Cream

- 3 LARGE EGGS
- 1 CUP HEAVY CREAM
- 1/2 TEASPOON SALT
- 1/4 TEASPOON FRESHLY GROUND BLACK PEPPER

Also called a Munster Valley Tourte, this two-crust tart is a rich, traditional main-dish meat pie from Alsace. At a copious Christmas holiday dinner, the tart might instead be served as an appetizer, followed by a fish course and then a roast. Featured on the menus of many auberges in the Alsatian countryside, particularly in the hilly, wooded Vosges region, the meat tart can be made with a combination of pork and either veal, rabbit, or duck, or with pork alone. This recipe, from André Renard, the award-winning pastry chef of Les Célébrités restaurant in the Essex House hotel in New York City, calls for just pork, in keeping with the way the tart was made in Chef Renard's hometown of Rambervillers, in the Vosges.

To make the tart: Combine the pork, parsley, onion, shallot, salt, pepper, oil, and wine in a medium mixing bowl. Stir well with a wooden spoon, then cover with plastic wrap and refrigerate a minimum of 4 hours or even overnight.

Preheat the oven to 400°F.

Fill the tart shell with the marinated meat mixture. Brush the edge of the bottom crust with some of the egg glaze. Cover the tart with the circle of dough and press the edges of the two crusts together firmly to seal, or crimp with a fork.

Cut a ½-inch hole in the center of the top crust with a sharp knife for the *cheminée*, or chimney, that will ventilate the tart. Make the *cheminée* by doubling over a 6-inch piece of aluminum foil, then folding up the open horizontal edge about half an inch and rolling the foil into a ½-inch-wide cigar. Insert it into the hole in the center of the crust. Score the crust lightly with a crosshatch (#) design, being careful not to cut through the dough. Brush the top with the remaining egg glaze and set on the middle rack of the oven. Reduce the temperature to 350°F and bake 55 minutes.

To make the cream: In a small mixing bowl, combine the eggs, cream, salt, and pepper and beat lightly. Using a funnel or small pitcher, pour the cream mixture carefully down the *cheminée*, letting the mixture flow into the tart little by little. Continue baking another 25 minutes, until the tart is a deep golden brown and the egg-and-cream filling has set. Remove to a wire rack and let rest for 10 minutes. Serve warm with a salad and, as Chef Renard suggests, a traditional Alsatian Sylvaner white wine. SERVES 6

Tartelettes Tatin du foie gras

FOIE GRAS–APPLE TARTLET TATIN

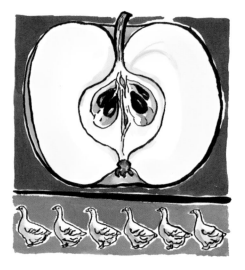

- 1 RECIPE PÂTE FEUILLETÉE RAPIDE (PAGE 21), ROLLED OUT 1/8-INCH THICK, OR 1 SHEET COMMERCIAL PUFF PASTRY, CHILLED BUT NOT FROZEN

- 4 3-OUNCE SLICES FRESH, RAW FOIE GRAS (FATTENED GOOSE OR DUCK LIVER)

- SALT AND FRESHLY GROUND BLACK PEPPER

- 3 TABLESPOONS UNSALTED BUTTER

- 2 GRANNY SMITH APPLES, PEELED, CORED, AND CUT INTO THIN SLICES

- 1/4 CUP ARMAGNAC OR OTHER BRANDY, SUCH AS COGNAC OR CALVADOS

- 2 TABLESPOONS HEAVY CREAM

Chief among the gastronomic riches of the Quercy region in France's southwest is the magnificent *foie gras*, made from either fattened goose or duck livers. The *foie gras* appears in many guises on regional menus— *au naturel*, in *terrines* or *pâtés*, poached in sweet wine, paired with artichoke hearts and truffles, in salads, and as stuffing for game birds, to note just a few. I love *foie gras* almost any way I find it, and was particularly taken with these Tatin-style tartlets the first time I had them several years ago at a rustic inn in Quercy. As special-occasion appetizer tarts, they're a fabulous beginning to a festive Christmas dinner.

Preheat the oven to 375°F.

Using an inverted teacup or a cookie cutter as a guide, cut four 4-inch circles from the pastry. Set aside.

Season the slices of liver with salt and pepper. Melt 1 tablespoon of butter in a large skillet, then add the slices of liver and sauté over medium heat until they are golden brown on both sides, about 3 minutes per side. Transfer them to a paper towel to drain. Melt another tablespoon of butter in the skillet, then add the apple slices and sauté over medium heat until they are golden brown, about 3 minutes on each side. Transfer the apple slices to a plate. Reserve the skillet.

Line the bottoms and sides of four 3½-inch buttered individual tartlet pans or 4 ramequins with the apple slices. Place a slice of liver in the center of each tartlet. Cover each tartlet pan with a pastry circle and carefully seal the edges. Prick the pastry in several spots with a basting needle or the tip of a small sharp knife. Set the tartlets on a baking sheet, and bake in the center of the oven for 15 to 18 minutes, until the pastry is golden brown. Remove from the oven. Invert each tartlet and transfer to an individual serving plate, carefully removing the mold.

Set the skillet used for browning the apples and *foie gras* over medium heat and add the Armagnac. Reduce it by half, then stir in the cream. Whisk in small pieces of the remaining butter, ½ teaspoon salt, and ¼ teaspoon pepper. Remove from the heat and spoon the sauce equally over the tartlets. Serve immediately. SERVES 4

Sweet Tarts

Tartelettes aux abricots

APRICOT TARTLETS

- 6 4-INCH PÂTE SUCRÉE (PAGE 19) OR PÂTE FEUILLETÉE RAPIDE (PAGE 21) TARTLET SHELLS, UNBAKED, OR STORE-BOUGHT

- 1 RECIPE CRÈME PÂTISSIÈRE (PAGE 23)

- 12 FRESH APRICOTS, PITTED AND CUT INTO QUARTERS (OR USE CANNED WHOLE APRICOTS, DRAINED, PATTED DRY, PITTED, AND CUT INTO QUARTERS)

- 1/2 CUP CONFECTIONERS' SUGAR

In the warm and yeasty, male-dominated world of French *boulange*—bread-baking—Isabelle and Valérie Ganachaud are unique. Not only are they the sole pair of sisters to have earned the respected diploma of *Maître en Boulangerie* (Master Baker) from the Institut National de la Boulangerie in Rouen, they are also the only women to have done so. Isabelle and Valérie are an intensely loyal and complementary duo. Working side by side in their enticing Paris *boulangerie*, La Flûte Gana, the sisters turn out what many aficionados believe to be the best bread in town, as well as rustic, home-style *pâtisseries*, such as these apricot tartlets. The tartlets are also delicious when made with apples or plums.

Preheat oven to 375°F.

Fill each tartlet shell with about ¼ cup *crème pâtissière*. Arrange apricot slices, skin side down, on top of the cream, using about 2 apricots per tartlet. Dust tartlets with ¼ cup confectioners' sugar and place on the center rack of the oven. Bake 35 to 40 minutes, until the crust and the cut edges of the fruit are browned and the cream filling has set. Remove to a wire rack to cool. Unmold the tartlets, dust with the remaining confectioners' sugar, and serve at room temperature. SERVES 6

Tartes Normandes

NORMANDY APPLE TARTS

- 1 10 1/2-INCH PÂTE BRISÉE SHELL (PAGE 16), UNBAKED

- 4 POUNDS (ABOUT 8) GOLDEN DELICIOUS APPLES

- 8 TABLESPOONS (1 STICK) UNSALTED BUTTER

- 1/4 CUP WATER

- 3/4 CUP GRANULATED SUGAR

- 1 TEASPOON VANILLA EXTRACT

- 1/2 CUP CONFECTIONERS' SUGAR

Researching a book on Normandy several years ago gave me the wonderful opportunity to spend two months in this beautiful province, living in Deauville, the stylish seaside town in the *département* of Calvados. During my time in Normandy, a fertile region blanketed with apple orchards, I came to know and love many terrific apple dishes, particularly the distinctive apple tarts. This traditional version of the Normandy apple tart, with an apple compote filling topped by sliced apples, is the perfect recipe for anyone just beginning to develop a classic sweet tart repertoire.

Note: Golden Delicious apples range in color from pale green to butter yellow; for baking purposes, choose apples that are yellow-green in tone—the ones that are bright yellow are often too ripe and mealy.

Peel, core, and chop half of the apples into small pieces. In a large frying pan over medium heat, melt 4 tablespoons of the butter without letting it brown. Add the chopped apples, stirring to coat them well with butter. Reduce the heat to medium low and cook the apples for 10 minutes, stirring frequently. Add the water, stir to blend, and continue cooking the apples for 10 more minutes. Add the granulated sugar, stir to blend, and cook until the apples are very soft and golden, and all the moisture has evaporated, about another 10 minutes. Remove the pan from the heat, stir in the vanilla extract, cover with aluminum foil, and set aside.

Preheat the oven to 400°F.

Peel, core, and halve the remaining apples. Cut them into thin, even slices about ¼-inch thick. Spread the apple compote over the bottom of the pastry shell. Arrange the apple slices, one slightly overlapping the other, in tight concentric circles on top of the compote, working from the outside edge into the center, so that all the compote is covered with apples. Melt the remaining 4 tablespoons butter and spoon it over the apple slices, then sift ¼ cup of the confectioners' sugar evenly over the top of the tart. Bake for 50 minutes in the center of the oven. Sift the remaining confectioners' sugar over the tart and bake until the apple slices are browned and several have slightly blackened edges, another 5 to 8 minutes. Cool on a wire rack. Serve warm or at room temperature. SERVES 6 TO 8

Tarte Normande à la crème

NORMANDY APPLE AND CREAM TART

- 1 10 1/2-INCH PÂTE SABLÉE SHELL (PAGE 18), UNBAKED

- 4 LARGE GRANNY SMITH APPLES, PEELED, CORED, AND CUT INTO LARGE (APPROXIMATELY 1-INCH) CUBES

- 2 TABLESPOONS UNSALTED BUTTER, MELTED AND KEPT WARM

- 2/3 CUP SUGAR

- 4 LARGE EGGS

- 2/3 CUP CRÈME FRAÎCHE OR HEAVY CREAM

- 1 TEASPOON VANILLA EXTRACT

At the elegant Château de Blanville, a bed-and-breakfast extraordinaire in the little village of St.-Luperce a short drive from Chartres, Cordon Bleu–trained Lisa de Cossé-Brissac, countess, chef, and mother of three, offers her guests market-fresh feasts that take their inspiration from the abundant seasonal fare of the French countryside. In autumn, when mountains of just-picked apples dot the landscape of Normandy, Lisa prepares her favorite apple tart—this Tarte Normande made with Granny Smith apples and a golden custard cream filling.

Preheat the oven to 375°F.

In a large bowl, toss the apples with the

melted butter until they are well coated, then set aside. Combine ½ cup of the sugar and the eggs in the bowl of an electric mixer. Beat the sugar and eggs together until they are creamy and pale yellow. Add the cream and the vanilla extract and beat until the ingredients are well blended. Spread the apples evenly over the bottom of the tart shell. Pour in the cream mixture so that the apples are evenly covered and the cream fills the tart to just below the rim of the shell. Sprinkle the remaining sugar over the top of the tart. Set the tart on a baking sheet, and bake in the center of the oven for 35 to 45 minutes, until the batter is set, the apples are browned, and the crust is deep golden brown. Cool on a wire rack. Remove the side of the pan from the tart, and serve lukewarm or at room temperature. SERVES 6 TO 8

Tarte Catalane aux pommes

CATALAN APPLE TART

- 1 10 1/2-INCH PÂTE SUCRÉE SHELL (PAGE 19), UNBAKED

- 6 GOLDEN DELICIOUS APPLES, PEELED, CORED, AND CUT INTO QUARTERS

- 1/2 CUP (1 STICK) UNSALTED BUTTER, MELTED OVER LOW HEAT

- 2/3 CUP SUGAR

- 2 OUNCES SLIVERED ALMONDS, FINELY GROUND

*O*ne of the most tempting treats to catch your eye as you enter Cador, the nineteenth-century tearoom just a short walk from the Louvre, is the succulent-looking Catalan Apple Tart, with large chunks of apple baked under a sugary almond-butter coating. The aromas that fill your kitchen as this tart bakes are truly mouthwatering. Indeed, the most difficult part of the preparation is summoning the self-control necessary to allow this tart to cool to lukewarm before serving. Delicious on its own, it's absolutely fabulous with a lily-gilding dollop of French vanilla ice cream.

Preheat the oven to 375°F.

Arrange the apple slices in the tart shell, fitting them as snugly as possible to cover the bottom of the shell. Cut several of the apple slices into smaller pieces to fill any gaps. Mix the butter, sugar, and ground almonds in a small bowl. Spoon the mixture evenly over the apples. Bake the tart about 35 minutes, until the top is golden brown and the crust is a deeper golden brown. Cool on a wire rack and serve slightly warm or at room temperature.

SERVES 6 TO 8

Streusel aux pommes

ALSATIAN APPLE STREUSEL TART

- 5 GRANNY SMITH OR OTHER CRISP, TART APPLES, PEELED, CORED, AND CUT INTO 1/2-INCH CUBES

- 1 1/2 CUPS SUGAR

- 1/2 CUP DRIED CURRANTS

- 1/4 CUP DARK RUM

- 1 1/2 CUPS ALL-PURPOSE FLOUR

- 1 TEASPOON BAKING POWDER

- 1 TABLESPOON PLUS 2 TEASPOONS GROUND CINNAMON

- 3/4 CUP (1 1/2 STICKS) UNSALTED BUTTER, CUT INTO SMALL PIECES AND SOFTENED

- 1 LARGE EGG

- 1 TEASPOON VANILLA EXTRACT

This unusual Alsatian apple tart, made with a streusel crumb base in place of a traditional pastry shell, is a specialty of the Hostellerie du Cerf, a 250-year-old coach house inn on the road to Strasbourg in Marlenheim. The hostellerie's young chef, Michel Husser, is the fourth generation of his family to work at the inn, established in 1930 by his great-grandparents. An inventive chef with a light touch whose cuisine is deeply inspired by Alsatian regional cooking, Michel was instrumental in the hostellerie's being awarded its second Michelin star in 1987.

Combine the apples with ½ cup of the sugar in a large mixing bowl, stirring to coat the apples well with the sugar. Cover with plastic wrap and refrigerate for several hours or overnight. In a small bowl, combine the currants with the rum, cover with plastic wrap, and set aside as long as the apples macerate in the sugar.

In a large mixing bowl, combine the flour, baking powder, remaining 1 cup sugar, and the cinnamon, and stir with a wooden spoon to blend. Add the butter, egg, and vanilla extract and mix well. When the ingredients are blended, work the mixture together with your fingers so that it forms little crumbly balls. Cover with plastic wrap and chill for 30 minutes.

Preheat the oven to 375°F.

Spread two-thirds of the streusel mixture over the bottom and sides of a well-buttered 10-inch glass pie dish, pressing in the streusel to make it flat and even all over. Add the currants and rum to the bowl with the apples and stir to combine. Drain off the excess liquid, then spoon the apple mixture over the streusel so that the base is evenly coated. Scatter the remaining streusel crumb mixture over the top of the apples. Bake on the bottom rack of the oven for 35 minutes. Cool on a wire rack and serve lukewarm or cold with a dollop of *crème fraîche* or *crème anglaise* (page 24). SERVES 8

Tarte aux pommes meringuée

CARAMELIZED APPLE-MERINGUE TART

- 1 10 1/2-INCH PÂTE SUCRÉE SHELL (PAGE 19), PARTIALLY BAKED
- 1/2 CUP (1 STICK) UNSALTED BUTTER
- 4 POUNDS (ABOUT 8) GOLDEN DELICIOUS APPLES, PEELED, CORED, AND CUT INTO EIGHTHS
- 1 SCANT CUP LIGHT BROWN SUGAR OR TURBINADO SUGAR
- 3 TABLESPOONS CALVADOS OR KIRSCH
- 1 TEASPOON VANILLA EXTRACT
- 5 LARGE EGG WHITES
- 1 CUP PLUS 2 TABLESPOONS CONFECTIONERS' SUGAR
- 1/2 CUP PINE NUTS

René Bérard, chef-owner of the beguiling Provençal inn, the Hostellerie Bérard in La Cadière d'Azur, is an award-winning pastry chef who prides himself on the luscious finales to his dinners. One of the most popular desserts among devotees of the inn is this impressive caramelized apple tart topped with meringue and pine nuts.

Melt the butter in a large skillet over medium-low heat. Add the apple slices and stir to coat them with the butter. Sprinkle on the sugar and stir to blend. Cook slowly, stirring occasionally with a wooden spoon to prevent sticking or burning, until the apples are softened and lightly golden brown, about 20 minutes. Pour in the Calvados and ignite to burn off the alcohol. Remove from heat, stir in the vanilla extract, then cover and set aside in the pan for 15 minutes. Transfer to a bowl, cover with plastic wrap, and refrigerate.

Two hours before serving, fill the tart shell with the apple mixture, cover with plastic wrap, and set aside at room temperature.

Fifteen minutes before serving, preheat the oven to 375°F.

In the bowl of an electric mixer, beat the egg whites until they are white and frothy. Sprinkle in ½ cup confectioners' sugar. Beat until the egg whites begin to form firm peaks, then sprinkle in another ½ cup confectioners' sugar and beat another 1 to 2 minutes until the meringue holds stiff peaks.

Using a pastry bag, pipe the meringue in large rosettes, or spread with a spatula, over the top of the tart so that the apple mixture is completely covered. Sprinkle on the pine nuts and bake for 8 minutes. Sift on the remaining 2 tablespoons confectioners' sugar and bake another 2 minutes, until the meringue is very lightly browned. Serve immediately. SERVES 8

Tarte Tatin aux pommes et aux poires

CARAMELIZED APPLE AND PEAR TART

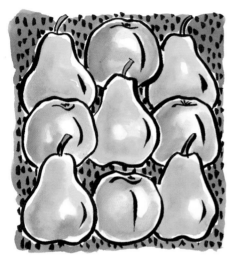

- 1 RECIPE PÂTE BRISÉE AU SUCRE (PAGE 17), OR PÂTE SABLÉE (PAGE 18)

- 6 TABLESPOONS UNSALTED BUTTER

- 1/2 CUP SUGAR

- 4 LARGE GRANNY SMITH OR GOLDEN DELICIOUS APPLES, PEELED, CORED, AND CUT INTO EIGHTHS

- 4 FIRM BOSC OR ANJOU PEARS, PEELED, CORED, AND QUARTERED

The creation of the traditional Tarte Tatin—a caramelized upside-down confection made with apples or, occasionally, pears—is credited to two nineteenth-century sisters named Tatin who worked at their family hotel in the Loire Valley village of Lamotte-Beuvron. But at the Château des Briottières, an aristocratic bed-and-breakfast in France's Anjou region, *châtelaine* Hedwige de Valbray, who does all the cooking, treats her autumn guests to a tart Tatin lush with both caramelized apples and pears.

Preheat the oven to 400°F.

Over medium heat, melt the butter in a glass stovetop-to-oven casserole (I use a 9-inch Pyrex Visions casserole, the better to see how the fruit is cooking and to prevent burning) or a deep cast-iron skillet. Sprinkle the sugar evenly over the bottom of the pan, then tightly pack in the apple and pear slices, alternating them, working from the outside edge of the pan in to the center. Fill any gaps with small slices of apple or pear. Cook over medium-low heat for about 20 minutes, until the butter caramelizes—thickening and turning a golden amber color. Shake the casserole or pan slightly from time to time to prevent sticking and, if you are using a glass casserole, check the bottom for burning. Remove from the heat.

Roll out the pastry on a floured work surface to a thickness of ⅛ inch, then, using a pot cover or upside-down tart tin as a guide, cut out a 10-inch circle. Lay the pastry circle on top of the apples and pears and tuck in the edges around the fruit inside the casserole or pan. Press the dough against the sides to seal. Bake in the center of the oven for 25 to 35 minutes, until the pastry is a deep golden brown. Cool on a wire rack for 10 minutes, then gently loosen the pastry and fruit with a metal spatula. Place a large serving plate top side down over the casserole or pan, invert the tart, and carefully transfer it—fruit side up—to the plate. Serve warm, accompanied by *crème fraîche* or vanilla ice cream. SERVES 6

Tartelettes aux poires

PEAR TARTLETS

Paris baker Jean-Luc Poujauran created this tart one afternoon using a new product he had picked up at Paris' organic market on the Left Bank—*confiture de lait*, a sweet, creamy spread made from a reduction of milk and sugar. In this recipe, condensed milk and brown sugar replace the unusual French spread.

- 1 RECIPE PÂTE SUCRÉE (PAGE 19)

- 1 CUP (1 14-OUNCE CAN) CONDENSED MILK

- 3 TABLESPOONS BROWN SUGAR

- 1 TEASPOON VANILLA EXTRACT

- 5 FIRM BUT RIPE BOSC OR BARTLETT PEARS, PEELED, CORED, AND DICED INTO 1/2-INCH CHUNKS

Roll out the pastry to a thickness of ⅛ inch on a floured work surface or on a sheet of plastic wrap, to prevent sticking. Using a small bowl, a teacup, or a pot cover as a guide, cut out six 5-inch circles. Press the dough into the bottom and up the sides of six buttered 3½-inch removable-bottom tartlet molds and smooth the edges along the top of each. Place the molds on a baking sheet, cover with plastic wrap, and set aside in a cool place.

Preheat the oven to 375°F.

Combine the condensed milk, brown sugar, and vanilla extract in a small saucepan. Warm the mixture over low heat until the sugar melts, about 2 minutes, stirring constantly so that the bottom doesn't brown and get lumpy. Set aside to cool to lukewarm.

In a large mixing bowl, combine the pears and milk mixture, stirring carefully with a spoon to coat the fruit well without bruising it. Spoon the coated fruit into the tartlet shells, filling each to the rim of the pan. Set the baking sheet with the tarts in the center of the oven and bake 35 to 40 minutes, until the tops of the tarts are nicely browned.

Remove the tartlets from the baking sheet and cool on a wire rack. When they are cool, carefully remove the tarts from the molds. Work very gently, since this pastry crust is crumbly, like a sugar cookie. It is certainly gilding the lily, but I love this tart with a scoop of vanilla ice cream. SERVES 6

Note: You can also make this tart in a 10½-inch tart pan rather than as individual tartlets. Simply increase the cooking time to 50 to 55 minutes.

Tarte aux poires chaudes

HOT PEAR TART

- 1 RECIPE PÂTE FEUILLETÉE RAPIDE (PAGE 21), ROLLED OUT INTO 11 X 14-INCH SHEETS, 1/8-INCH THICK, OR 2 SHEETS COMMERCIAL PUFF PASTRY, CHILLED BUT NOT FROZEN

- 4 TABLESPOONS SUGAR

- 4 FIRM PEARS, PREFERABLY ANJOU OR BOSC, PEELED, CORED, AND VERY THINLY SLICED

- JUICE OF 1 LEMON

- 4 TABLESPOONS (1/2 STICK) UNSALTED BUTTER, CUT INTO LITTLE BITS

If you have puff pastry dough on hand (I sometimes buy mine several sheets at a time from a good local bakery), this is one of the simplest tarts to make. You can accomplish everything, start to finish, in about 20 minutes. Not only is this tart delicious with pears, but it works equally well with apples, nectarines, blueberries, or raspberries. I must confess that I sometimes make this tart as a sybaritic breakfast treat with whatever fruit is on hand!

Preheat the oven to 400°F.

Using a pot cover or an inverted cereal bowl as a guide, cut out four 5½-inch circles of pastry. Transfer the circles to a lightly greased baking sheet. Sprinkle 1 teaspoon of sugar over each pastry circle.

Toss the pear slices with the lemon juice. On each tart, arrange the slices from one pear in an overlapping circular pattern, working from the outside in, leaving a ½-inch border at the edge. Scatter 1 tablespoon of butter over each tart, then sprinkle the remaining sugar equally over the 4 tarts. Bake on the center rack of the oven for about 18 minutes, until the pastry is golden brown and the fruit is slightly caramelized and bubbly. Serve immediately. SERVES 4

Note: To make this tart with other fruit, or to make single portions, use 1 sliced fruit or ½ cup of berries, 1 tablespoon butter, and 1 tablespoon sugar per tart.

Tarte aux framboises provençale

PROVENÇAL RASPBERRY TART

For the Crust

- 1 1/4 CUP ALL-PURPOSE FLOUR
- 8 TABLESPOONS (1 STICK) UNSALTED BUTTER, CHILLED AND CUT INTO BITS
- 1/4 CUP SUGAR
- 1/4 TEASPOON SALT
- 1/2 CUP GROUND BLANCHED ALMONDS
- 1 MEDIUM EGG
- 1 TABLESPOON EXTRA-LIGHT OLIVE OIL

For the Filling

- 3/4 CUP SUGAR
- ZEST OF 1 LEMON
- 1 TEASPOON BAKING POWDER
- 1 CUP ALL-PURPOSE FLOUR
- 1 CUP HALF-AND-HALF
- 1/4 CUP EXTRA-LIGHT OLIVE OIL
- 2 LARGE EGGS
- 3 TABLESPOONS MELTED BUTTER
- 1/2 POUND (ABOUT 2 SCANT CUPS) RASPBERRIES
- 1/4 CUP CONFECTIONERS' SUGAR

At the Château du Domaine St.-Martin, an idyllic hilltop inn set in the sun-washed, herb-scented countryside of Vence, Chef Dominique Ferrière prepares memorable Provençal cuisine from the Domaine's own fruits, vegetables, eggs, and olive oil. Meals are served in the bay-windowed dining room, with its panoramic views of the Mediterranean far below. One particularly tempting dessert is this delightful raspberry tart, with plump raspberries nestled in a flanlike cream delicately flavored with almonds and a touch of light olive oil.

To make the crust: In a food processor or a medium mixing bowl, combine the flour, butter, sugar, salt, and almonds. Process for about 12 seconds, or mash with your fingertips, until the mixture is dry and crumbly, resembling coarse cornmeal. Add the egg and olive oil and pulse, 10 or 12 times, or mix, until the dough comes together but before it forms a ball. Remove the dough from the bowl and, with lightly floured hands, knead between your palms for about 1 minute. Press flat into a disk, wrap with plastic wrap, and refrigerate for at least 1 hour.

On a well-floured work surface, roll out the dough to a 12-inch circle, about ⅛-inch thick. Transfer the pastry to a buttered, 9½-inch removable-bottom tart pan and press into the bottom and fluted sides, leaving ½ inch excess dough extending above the rim; fold this ½ inch of dough over onto itself, creating a doubled ¼-inch border. Flute the edges with your thumb and forefinger. Prick the bottom of the shell, cover with plastic wrap, and refrigerate for half an hour.

Preheat the oven to 375°F.

Remove shell from the refrigerator, discard plastic wrap, and cover with aluminum foil. Fill shell with baking weights such as dried beans or rice, then bake in the center of the oven for 8 minutes. Remove weights and aluminum foil and bake for another 8 minutes. Set on a wire rack to cool.

To make the filling: In the bowl of an electric mixer, combine the sugar, lemon zest, baking powder, and flour. Mix gently to blend. Add the half-and-half and olive oil and mix to blend. Add the eggs and melted butter and mix until the ingredients form a smooth batter.

Spread the raspberries evenly in the baked shell. Pour in the batter and fill to ¼ inch below the top of the shell. Bake in the center of the oven for 33 to 36 minutes, until the filling just starts to brown and the center of the tart is firm when the pan is jiggled. Remove from the oven and sprinkle with the confectioners' sugar. Cool and serve at room temperature. SERVES 6

Tarte soufflée aux framboises

RASPBERRY TART WITH CARAMELIZED CREAM

- 1 10 1/2-INCH PÂTE SUCRÉE SHELL (PAGE 19), UNBAKED
- 12 OUNCES (ABOUT 3 CUPS) RASPBERRIES

For the Almond Cream
- 4 TABLESPOONS (1/2 STICK) UNSALTED BUTTER, CUT INTO BITS AND SOFTENED
- 1/3 CUP SUGAR
- 1 LARGE EGG
- 1/2 CUP SLIVERED ALMONDS, GROUND TO A POWDER

For the Crème Chiboust
- 4 LARGE EGG WHITES
- 1 1/3 CUPS SUGAR
- 1/4 CUP WATER
- 1 PACKET (7 GRAMS) UNFLAVORED GELATIN
- 1 RECIPE CRÈME PÂTISSIÈRE (PAGE 23), FRESHLY MADE AND STILL WARM, USING 4 EGG YOLKS INSTEAD OF 3

This elaborate special-occasion tart from *pâtissier* Alain Jacq at La Réserve de Beaulieu is a completely seductive confection. It combines plump fresh raspberries with sugared almond-butter and is crowned with a fluffy layer of caramelized pastry cream that resembles nothing so much as a *crème brûlée*. Because the pastry cream variation, called a *crème Chiboust* after the nineteenth-century pastry chef who developed it, is a somewhat demanding combination of Italian meringue and *crème pâtissière*, this is not a tart for beginners. For the confident cook, however, this tart should present no problems, and will well reward the effort put into creating it. It is sublime!

Note: As is the case with many *pâtisseries*, this tart is much better when served without being refrigerated, so plan to prepare it an hour or two beforehand.

Preheat the oven to 375°F.

Line the tart shell with aluminum foil, then fill with dried beans, rice, or baking weights. Set on the center rack of the oven and bake 8 minutes.

To make the almond cream: Combine the butter and sugar in the bowl of an electric mixer and beat until blended and pale yellow, about 1 minute. Add the egg and the almond powder and beat at medium speed for 4 minutes, scraping down the sides of the bowl from time to time, until the mixture is smooth and fluffy.

After the tart shell has baked 8 minutes, remove the beans and the foil. Spread the almond cream over the bottom of the tart shell, covering it completely, return to the oven and bake about 15 minutes, until the crust and the almond cream are nicely browned. Set aside on a wire rack to cool.

To make the crème Chiboust: In the bowl of an electric mixer, beat the egg whites until they are very firm but not stiff. In a small saucepan, combine 1 cup sugar, the water, and gelatin. Stir to blend. Set over low heat and bring to a boil without stirring. Continue boiling, still without stirring, until the temperature on a candy thermometer dipped into the syrup reaches 248°F, or, if you are not using a candy thermometer, about 7 minutes. Remove from the heat. Resume beating the egg whites and carefully pour the sugar syrup directly onto them—try to avoid getting the syrup on the side of the mixing bowl, where it will stick. Continue beating until the meringue is cool and very stiff, about 4 or 5 minutes.

Preheat the broiler.

Fold one-third of the meringue into the *crème pâtissière*. Fold carefully, to maintain as much air and volume as possible. Fold in the next third of the meringue, and finally the last third, until the *crème pâtissière* and meringue are completely blended.

Spoon the raspberries into the tart shell, then spread the *crème Chiboust* evenly over the top of the tart, smoothing the surface with a metal spatula or, if you have one, a palette knife. Sprinkle the remaining ⅓ cup sugar evenly over the top of the tart and set under the broiler for about 1 minute, until the sugar caramelizes to a deep golden brown. Remove immediately and set on a wire rack to cool. Serve at room temperature. SERVES 6 TO 8

Tarte aux figues, coulis de figues du vin rouge

FRESH FIG TART WITH RED-WINE-AND-FIG SAUCE

For the Sauce

- 2 CUPS RED BURGUNDY OR PINOT NOIR WINE
- 4 FRESH PURPLE FIGS
- 1/2 CUP GRANULATED SUGAR
- 1 CINNAMON STICK

For the Tart

- 1 RECIPE PÂTE FEUILLETÉE RAPIDE (PAGE 21), ROLLED OUT TO A 10 X 15-INCH RECTANGLE, 1/8-INCH THICK, OR 2 SHEETS COMMERCIAL PUFF PASTRY, CHILLED BUT NOT FROZEN
- 1/3 CUP CONFECTIONERS' SUGAR
- 12 FRESH PURPLE FIGS
- 3 TABLESPOONS UNSALTED BUTTER, CUT INTO SMALL BITS
- 3 TABLESPOONS GRANULATED SUGAR

Bernard Loiseau, one of France's newest three-star chefs, is a wizard at creating fantastic desserts at his Burgundy restaurant, La Côte d'Or, in Saulieu. Some are variations of traditional French country desserts. One example is this Tarte aux Figues. "A classic way of serving fresh figs," Loiseau says, "is to poach them in red wine. In this recipe, I present instead a tart topped with lightly baked figs, surrounded by a sauce of figs that have been macerated and then cooked in red wine."

***

Note: Make the sauce first, 24 hours in advance.

To make the sauce: Heat the wine in a saucepan to very hot but not boiling. Remove from the heat, tip the pan slightly,

then hold a lighted match close to the surface of the wine. When the flame dies away, set aside to cool, then transfer to a bowl. Cut the figs into small pieces and add to the wine. Cover with plastic wrap and refrigerate overnight.

The next day, combine the wine and fig mixture with the sugar and cinnamon stick in a saucepan. Cook slowly over medium heat until the wine is reduced by half. Remove from the heat, take out the cinnamon stick, and pour the mixture into a food processor or blender and puree. Pour the mixture through a strainer into a bowl, pressing the figs with the back of a large spoon. Cover with plastic wrap and refrigerate.

Preheat the oven to 400°F.

To make the tart: Using a pastry brush, lightly moisten a baking sheet with water. Lay out the sheet (or sheets) of puff pastry on the baking sheet and bake for 12 to 15 minutes, until the pastry is puffed and golden brown. Let cool, then, using a 5- or

5½-inch pot cover or inverted cereal bowl as a guide, cut the pastry into 4 circles. Set the oven on broil. Remove the excess dough, sprinkle the circles with half the confectioners' sugar, and set under the broiler for 1 minute. Remove and set aside.

Just before serving, preheat the oven to 400°F. Cut the figs into quarters, cutting almost but not quite all the way through, and place them on a buttered baking sheet. Place about 1 teaspoon of butter bits atop each fig and sprinkle the figs evenly with the granulated sugar. Bake 7 minutes. Remove from oven and set on a wire rack.

Spread a circle of sauce slightly larger than the tart across the bottom of each dessert plate. Set the tart circles on top of the sauce. Atop each tart, arrange 3 figs in a pinwheel fashion, setting the second fig over the first in the spaces between the quarters, then the third between the quarters of the second. Drizzle the tarts with the remaining sauce, dust with the remaining confectioners' sugar, and serve immediately. SERVES 4

Tarte aux raisins château Lagrezette

CHÂTEAU LAGREZETTE'S GRAPE TART

- 1 10 1/2-INCH PÂTE BRISÉE AU SUCRE SHELL (PAGE 17), UNBAKED

- 1 3/4 POUNDS (ABOUT 3 1/2 CUPS) SEEDLESS RED GRAPES

- 1/4 CUP KIRSCH OR OTHER EAU-DE-VIE (FRAMBOISE, POIRE WILLIAM)

- 2/3 CUP CONFECTIONERS' SUGAR

- 2 LARGE EGGS PLUS 1 YOLK

- 3/4 CUP CRÈME FRAÎCHE OR HEAVY CREAM

- 1/4 CUP HALF-AND-HALF

- 1/2 TEASPOON SALT

- 1/4 CUP WHOLE UNBLANCHED ALMONDS, FINELY GROUND

In the rustic and beautiful wine country of Cahors in southwest France, Château Lagrezette sits surrounded by lush vineyards producing the region's signature Malbec, Merlot, and Tannat grapes. One of the premier wine producers of Cahors, Lagrezette, a handsome Renaissance château, is the setting for festive family reunions and frequent feasts with assorted relatives and friends. I still remember fondly the al fresco lunch I enjoyed with owners Alain-Dominique and Marie-Thérèse Perrin on a sunny day in early May several years ago. The meal began with silky slices of local *foie gras*, continued with roast lamb and several vintages of Lagrezette's rich, distinctive red wines, and finished, appropriately enough, with this luscious grape tart.

Wash the grapes, place in a medium bowl, add the kirsch, and sprinkle on ⅓ cup confectioners' sugar. Stir gently to mix, then set aside to macerate 1 hour.

Preheat the oven to 375°F.

In a large mixing bowl, whisk together the eggs and egg yolk, *crème fraîche*, half-and-half, salt, and remaining confectioners' sugar, reserving 1 tablespoon. Add the almonds and whisk to blend. Drain the grapes, add the grape liquid to the cream mixture, and stir to blend. Spread the cream mixture over the bottom of the tart shell. Arrange the grapes on top of the cream and bake 40 to 45 minutes, until the cream filling has set, the crust has browned, and the top has partially browned. Remove tart from oven, sprinkle with the reserved tablespoon of confectioners' sugar, and cool on a wire rack. Serve at room temperature. SERVES 6

Pain perdu aux quetches

FRENCH TOAST PLUM TART

- 1 LOAF CHALLAH OR LONG BRIOCHE BREAD
- 3 LARGE EGGS
- 1/2 TEASPOON VANILLA EXTRACT
- 3 TABLESPOONS CONFECTIONERS' SUGAR
- 1/3 CUP GRANULATED SUGAR
- 1/4 TEASPOON GROUND CINNAMON
- 3 TABLESPOONS QUICK-COOKING TAPIOCA
- 3 POUNDS RED ITALIAN PLUMS, HALVED AND PITTED

This unusual tart, wonderful as a brunch dish, actually came to me in a dream (a sure sign of excessive tart research!). My inspiration, I'm certain, was a fanciful home-style dessert conceived by Paris baker Jean-Luc Poujauran, in which small baked apples filled with jam were served atop rounds of warm French toast. In this "dream tart," the traditional pastry crust is replaced by a base of bread slices dipped in vanilla-flavored egg batter, then topped with plums and sugar. It bakes up big, puffy, and delicious . . . in fact, I must say, just like a dream come true!

Preheat the oven to 400°F.

Trim the crust from the bread, then cut into 1/2-inch slices.

In a mixing bowl, combine the eggs, vanilla extract, and 2 tablespoons confectioners' sugar. Whisk to blend. Dip the slices of bread into the egg mixture until they are saturated, then arrange across the bottom and up along the sides of a buttered 10-inch glass pie dish, fitting the slices snugly together so that the dish is completely covered, with no gaps.

Mix the granulated sugar and cinnamon in a small bowl. Sprinkle 3 tablespoons of the sugar mixture and 2 tablespoons of the tapioca over the bread slices. Arrange the plums skin side down over the bread base, fitting the fruit snugly with as little space as possible left uncovered. Fill in any gaps with small bits and pieces of plum, and sprinkle the remaining tapioca on top.

Bake tart in the center of the oven for 25 minutes. Lower the temperature to 350°F and bake another 15 minutes, until the tart is browned and puffy. Dust with remaining confectioners' sugar, cool slightly on a wire rack, then serve warm. SERVES 6

Tarte au rhum Toulouse-Lautrec

TOULOUSE-LAUTREC'S BUTTER-RUM TART

- 1 RECIPE PÂTE SUCRÉE (PAGE 19)
  OR PÂTE SABLÉE (PAGE 18)

- 4 TABLESPOONS UNSALTED BUTTER,
  CHILLED AND CUT INTO BITS

- 1/4 CUP SUGAR

- 3 TABLESPOONS DARK RUM

Toulouse-Lautrec was as passionate a cook as he was a painter. He loved entertaining his friends at home, preparing lavish dinners that began with extravagant cocktails he called "potions" and went on to multiple courses washed down with rivers of wine and topped off by easy-to-prepare desserts plus a touch of brandy. He collected and created recipes throughout his life. After he died in 1901, his great friend and fellow artist Maurice Joynant gathered his recipes together in a book, accompanied by Lautrec's scribbles and sketches. This recipe for Lautrec's rum tart is extremely simple to prepare and takes only minutes from start to finish. It doesn't really resemble a tart . . . more like a giant, buttery, rum-soaked cookie.

Preheat the oven to 500°F.

Roll out the dough on a floured work surface to a thickness of ¼ inch. Using a plate or an upside-down tart pan as a guide, cut out a 10-inch circle of dough. Lay the dough into a well-buttered 10-inch glass pie dish. In this tart, the dough does not come all the way up the sides of the dish but should cover the bottom and come just slightly up the sides, about ½ inch— similar in appearance to a pizza pie crust.

Fold the excess dough over onto itself to make a double-thick border. Cover with plastic wrap and refrigerate for 15 minutes.

Scatter the butter evenly over the dough. Sprinkle the sugar over the butter. Spoon the rum evenly over the sugar. Bake in the center of the oven for 12 minutes, until the tart is browned and bubbly. Cool for 5 minutes, then serve. This little tart is absolutely decadent served with rich vanilla or coffee ice cream. SERVES 6

Tarte au chocolat Gérard Mulot

GÉRARD MULOT'S CHOCOLATE TART

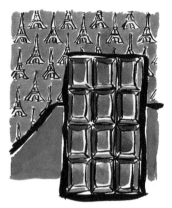

For the Crust

- 12 TABLESPOONS (1 1/2 STICKS) UNSALTED BUTTER, SOFTENED
- 3/4 CUP CONFECTIONERS' SUGAR
- 2 LARGE EGGS
- 1/2 TEASPOON SALT
- 2 TEASPOONS VANILLA SUGAR, OR 1/2 TEASPOON VANILLA EXTRACT
- 2 CUPS ALL-PURPOSE FLOUR
- 5 TABLESPOONS IMPORTED UNSWEETENED COCOA
- 1 OUNCE SLIVERED ALMONDS, FINELY GROUND (ABOUT 1/4 CUP)

For the Filling

- 14 OUNCES (2 LARGE BARS) COFFEE-FLAVORED BITTERSWEET DARK CHOCOLATE, OR 14 OUNCES BITTERSWEET DARK CHOCOLATE AND 2 TEASPOONS INSTANT COFFEE
- 1 CUP HEAVY CREAM
- 1/3 CUP (5 1/3 TABLESPOONS) UNSALTED BUTTER, SOFTENED

With its dark cocoa crust and its intense, voluptuous chocolate filling, this is one of the richest tarts I've ever tasted. It is among the most popular specialties of elite Paris *pâtissier* Gérard Mulot, whose Left Bank shop caters to Catherine Deneuve, many Latin Quarter publishers, and the pastry-loving members of the nearby French Sénat. The confection should be made with the very best chocolate you can find—preferably Valrhona (see mail-order sources, page 124) or imported brands such as Lindt, Godiva, or Perugina. The tart is still excellent when made with supermarket brands, but it doesn't quite reach the to-die-for heights attained with Valrhona chocolate.

Note: The crust should be prepared at least 12 hours before baking.

To make the crust: In a food processor or an electric mixer, blend the butter, confectioners' sugar, eggs, salt, and vanilla sugar or extract, processing about 10 seconds. Add the flour, cocoa, and almonds to the processor or mixing bowl and pulse 5 or 6 times, or mix, just to blend. Remove the dough from the bowl, press it into a flat disk, wrap well in plastic wrap, and refrigerate at least 12 hours.

On a floured surface, roll out the chilled dough to an 11-inch circle about ⅛-inch thick. Transfer the dough to a buttered 9-inch tart pan or pie dish. Press the dough in gently so that ¼ inch extends above the rim of the pan, then flute the edge with your fingers. Prick the bottom of the shell with a fork, cover with plastic wrap, and chill for at least 2 hours.

Preheat the oven to 350°F.

Bake the tart shell on the center rack of the oven for 20 minutes. Cool on a wire rack.

To make the filling: Chop the chocolate into little pieces and place in a mixing bowl. (If you are using instant coffee, sprinkle it in over the chocolate.) In a small saucepan, heat the cream just to the point of boiling, then pour it over the chocolate. With a wooden spoon, slowly and gently stir the mixture until the chocolate and cream are blended. Try to avoid creating air bubbles. Let cool until the mixture is lukewarm but still liquid.

Gently stir the butter into the chocolate until blended. Pour the chocolate mixture into the tart shell, filling it to just below the brim, almost but not quite to the point of overflowing. Set aside in a cool, but not cold, place (not the refrigerator) for at least 4 hours. The tart, as Gérard Mulot advises, "should be served firm but unctuous."

SERVES 6 TO 8

Tarte au chocolat infusé au basilic

CHOCOLATE-BASIL TART, WITH
GRAPEFRUIT-ROSEMARY-HONEY SAUCE

For the Tart

- 1 9 1/2-INCH PÂTE SUCRÉE SHELL (PAGE 19), PARTIALLY BAKED
- 1/3 CUP MILK
- 1 CUP HEAVY CREAM
- 1 BUNCH (ABOUT 1 CUP LOOSELY PACKED) FRESH BASIL
- 1/2 POUND BITTERSWEET DARK CHOCOLATE, PREFERABLY VALRHONA, PERUGINA, OR LINDT, BROKEN INTO SMALL PIECES
- 1 LARGE EGG, BEATEN
- 2 TABLESPOONS UNSALTED BUTTER, SOFTENED
- 6 SPRIGS OF BASIL, FOR GARNISH

For the Sauce

- 2 PINK GRAPEFRUITS, PEELED, SECTIONED, FLESH SEPARATED FROM MEMBRANES
- 3 TABLESPOONS HONEY
- 1 SPRIG FRESH OR DRIED ROSEMARY
- 1 TEASPOON CORNSTARCH

With its amazing combination of flavors, this tart conveys the essence of being on the beguiling Riviera island of Porquerolles, where heather, mimosa, lavender, and wild herbs bloom with abandon. Chef Joel Guillet, from the Mas du Langoustier at the island's southwestern tip, uses grace notes of basil, wild rosemary, and native honey to complement the intense flavor of chocolate in a unique and distinctive way.

Preheat the oven to 325°F.

To make the tart: Combine the milk, cream, and basil in a saucepan. Bring to a boil, then remove immediately from the heat. Set aside 5 minutes to let the flavor of the basil infuse the cream mixture.

Strain the cream mixture into a large bowl and discard the basil. Add the chocolate to the bowl and stir with a wooden spoon until the chocolate is blended and the mixture is thick and silky. Add the egg and butter to the chocolate mixture and stir well to blend. Pour into the tart shell, set on the center rack of the oven, and bake for 20 minutes. Remove to a wire rack and let cool.

To make the sauce: Remove any remaining seeds or membranes from the grapefruit sections. In a shallow dish to catch the juice, chop the grapefruit into small bits.

Combine the fruit and juice with the honey and rosemary in a medium saucepan. Bring to a boil, then reduce the heat to a simmer. In a small cup, combine the cornstarch with 3 tablespoons of the sauce, stirring to blend. Pour back into the fruit sauce and stir until thickened. Remove from the heat, transfer to a bowl, and set aside to cool. Remove rosemary and discard. Cover the sauce and refrigerate until ready to serve. Serve lukewarm with the chilled sauce spooned around each slice on the individual dessert plates. Garnish each serving with a sprig of basil, if you wish. SERVES 6

Tartelettes au chocolat noir amer et aux noisettes

BITTERSWEET CHOCOLATE AND HAZELNUT TARTLETS

- 6 4-INCH PÂTE SUCRÉE SHELLS (PAGE 19), PARTIALLY BAKED
- 1 CUP WHOLE HAZELNUTS, SKINS REMOVED
- 6 OUNCES (2 3-OUNCE BARS OR BULK CHOCOLATE) BITTERSWEET DARK CHOCOLATE
- 6 TABLESPOONS (3/4 STICK) UNSALTED BUTTER, CUT INTO PIECES
- 1/3 CUP SUGAR
- 3 TABLESPOONS ALL-PURPOSE FLOUR
- ZEST (ABOUT 1 TABLESPOON) OF 1/2 ORANGE
- 2 TABLESPOONS GRAND MARNIER OR OTHER ORANGE-FLAVORED LIQUEUR
- 2 LARGE EGGS
- 2 TABLESPOONS IMPORTED UNSWEETENED COCOA

One of the dazzling finales to a meal at the three-star Le Louis XV restaurant in Monte Carlo is master chef Alain Ducasse's bittersweet chocolate tartlet, fragrant with the essence of orange and crunchy with grilled hazelnuts. A brilliant chef, Ducasse composes with flavors and textures the way Matisse created with color and line: always with an eye to the elemental. The results at Le Louis XV, and at Ducasse's eponymous new restaurant in Paris, are always absolutely original and a delight to the palate.

———

Preheat the broiler.

Spread the hazelnuts on a baking sheet, then set them under the broiler for a minute or two, until they are lightly browned. Set aside to cool. Reserve 18 nuts for garnish, then coarsely chop the remaining nuts and set aside.

Preheat the oven to 350°F.

Melt 4 ounces (1⅓ bars) of the chocolate in a double boiler, then set aside, keeping the chocolate over the hot water. Combine the butter and sugar in a large, heavy-bottomed saucepan. Set over medium-low heat and, stirring constantly, melt the butter and sugar, being very careful not to let them brown. Stir in the flour, orange zest, orange liqueur, eggs, and melted chocolate. When blended, stir in the hazelnuts and remove from the heat. Spoon the chocolate filling into the tartlet shells, set on the center rack of the oven, and bake 10 to 12 minutes, just until the filling sets. The center of the tart should remain creamy and unctuous. Set on a wire rack to cool slightly.

Place each tartlet on an individual serving dish. Grate the remaining chocolate over each tart, dust the tarts and plates with the cocoa, garnish with the reserved hazelnuts, and serve warm or lukewarm. SERVES 6

Tarte chaude au chocolat amer

WARM DARK CHOCOLATE TART WITH PISTACHIO SAUCE

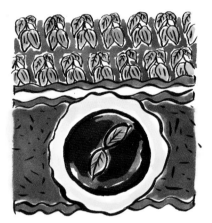

For the Sauce

- 3 OUNCES (ABOUT 3/4 CUP) SHELLED PISTACHIO NUTS
- 1 TABLESPOON CORNSTARCH
- 1 TABLESPOON CONFECTIONERS' SUGAR
- 3 CUPS MILK
- 5 LARGE EGG YOLKS
- 2/3 CUPS GRANULATED SUGAR

For the Tart

- 1/4 POUND BITTERSWEET DARK CHOCOLATE, PREFERABLY IMPORTED, SUCH AS VALRHONA, PERUGINA, OR LINDT, BROKEN INTO SMALL PIECES
- 1/2 CUP (1 STICK) UNSALTED BUTTER, CUT INTO PIECES
- 2 TABLESPOONS UNSWEETENED COCOA
- 4 LARGE EGGS, SEPARATED
- 3/4 CUP GRANULATED SUGAR
- 1/4 CUP ESPRESSO OR VERY STRONG COFFEE
- 1/2 CUP MINT LEAVES, FOR GARNISH

This celestially light, intensely chocolate confection from two-star Paris chef Michel Rostang, created from two layers of chocolate meringue cooked in two stages, is hardly a tart in the traditional sense. An exterior fragile and delicately crispy with the barely resistant quality of a quail's eggshell, envelops a warm, soft, and unctuous interior, and the first layer of meringue fills the role of a conventional pastry crust. But if Michel Rostang calls it a tart, I call it a tart. When I first served it to a gathering of friends, one neighborhood gourmand announced, "This, and I'm not kidding, is the best chocolate dessert I have ever tasted!"

Note: This is not a dessert that can be prepared well ahead of time. Begin preparations 2 to 3 hours before serving.

Line a baking sheet with kitchen parchment. Grease the top of the parchment with softened butter. Butter a 9-inch tart ring (not a pan but a bottomless metal circle) or the sides of a 9-inch springform pan (you will not be using the bottom) and set it in the center of the lined baking sheet.

Preheat the oven to 425°F.

To make the sauce: Place the pistachio nuts in a small saucepan, cover with cold water, and bring to a boil over high heat. Reduce to a low boil and cook for 8 minutes. Drain, then remove all traces of skin from the nuts. Combine the nuts with the cornstarch and confectioners' sugar in the small bowl of a food processor. Pulse several times, then stir the ingredients. Pulse and stir several times more, until the ingredients form a rough paste. Transfer to a small bowl, cover, and refrigerate until ready to use.

Combine the milk and pistachio paste in a medium saucepan, then bring to a boil over medium heat. While the milk mixture is heating, combine the egg yolks and granulated sugar in a medium bowl. Whisk until the mixture is completely blended and pale yellow in color. Pour in about ½ cup of the hot milk mixture into the eggs and stir with a whisk to blend. Pour this back into the saucepan with the milk mixture, reduce heat to low, and heat slowly, stirring constantly with a wooden spoon until the sauce thickens and coats the back of the spoon. Do not let the mixture come to a boil, as this sauce can separate in a flash and no amount of stirring can rectify it. Remove from the heat and pour the sauce into a pitcher or sauceboat through a fine strainer. Cover and refrigerate until ready to use.

To make the tart: Melt the chocolate, butter, and cocoa in a double boiler set over medium heat. Stir, remove from the heat, and set aside. With an electric mixer, beat the egg whites until they are almost firm, forming soft peaks. Sprinkle in the

granulated sugar and beat until the egg whites form stiff peaks, then set aside. Using a whisk, gently stir the egg yolks and espresso into the melted chocolate mixture until blended. Using a rubber spatula, slowly and gently fold the chocolate mixture little by little into the egg whites, maintaining as much volume as possible.

Pour half the chocolate mixture into the tart ring. Bake in the center of the oven for 10 minutes. Remove and set on a wire rack to cool for about 15 minutes. Then pour the remaining chocolate mixture into the cooked ring, cover with plastic wrap, and refrigerate until just before serving.

Preheat the oven to 425°F.

Bake the tart in the center of the oven for 12 minutes, until the top is puffed and slightly resistant. Remove to a wire rack. Run a spatula around the inside edge of the tart ring, then unmold immediately and carefully transfer to a serving dish. Serve immediately. Present each slice surrounded by the pistachio sauce and garnished with a sprig of mint. SERVES 6

Tarte au citron meringuée

LEMON MERINGUE TART

- 1 10 1/2-INCH PÂTE SUCRÉE SHELL (PAGE 19), PARTIALLY BAKED TO A VERY PALE GOLD

- 2/3 CUP (ABOUT 4 LEMONS) FRESH LEMON JUICE

- 1/2 CUP (1 STICK) UNSALTED BUTTER, CUT INTO SMALL BITS

- 6 LARGE EGGS, SEPARATED, PLUS 1 WHOLE EGG

- 1 1/2 CUPS GRANULATED SUGAR

- 2 TABLESPOONS SIFTED CAKE FLOUR

- 1 CUP CONFECTIONERS' SUGAR

- PINCH OF SALT

Les Nuits des Thés is one of the most chic and discreet tearooms in Paris. Tucked behind the facade of a venerable 1930s *boulangerie*, this serene Left Bank oasis sits just one block from the Seine and two from the Boulevard Saint-Germain in an area chockablock with art galleries and antique dealers. The soft neutral decor, highlighted by owner Jacqueline Cedelle's collection of antique teapots, forms the perfect setting for an intimate *tête-à-tête* over a light lunch or afternoon tea. An elegant and *soigné* clientele of gallery owners, antique dealers, and shoppers fill the tables. The first tart I had here, one rainy winter afternoon, was this lovely lemon tart crowned with a sweet meringue, delicious with a pot of Les Nuits des Thés' vanilla-scented tea.

Preheat the oven to 300°F.

Heat the lemon juice and butter in a large saucepan over medium heat just until the butter melts. Remove from the heat.

Combine the egg yolks, whole egg, and 1 cup granulated sugar in the bowl of an electric mixer, then beat about 2 minutes, until the mixture is smooth and pale yellow. Add the flour and beat a few seconds, until blended. Pour the egg mixture into the saucepan with the butter and lemon juice, and stir well with a wooden spoon to blend.

Return the pan to the burner and cook over medium heat, stirring constantly so that the bottom doesn't burn, just until the mixture almost comes to a simmer and has thickened so that it coats the back of the spoon, about 3 minutes. If the mixture starts to get lumpy and curdlike, remove from the heat immediately and whisk briskly to smooth the mixture. Pour the lemon filling into the tart shell

and bake on the center rack of the oven 12 to 15 minutes, until the filling has set but has not browned. Remove to a wire rack and let cool.

Increase the oven temperature to 375°F. In the bowl of an electric mixer, beat the egg whites until white and frothy. Add half the confectioners' sugar and ¼ cup of the granulated sugar and continue beating until the egg whites are almost firm, about 2 minutes. Add the remaining confectioners' and granulated sugar and the salt. Beat another 2 to 3 minutes, until the egg whites are very firm and can form and hold stiff peaks.

If you have a pastry bag with a star-shaped nozzle, use it to pipe the meringue topping over the lemon filling, carefully covering the whole top from the edge of the crust to the center. At Les Nuits des Thés, the chef pipes the meringue in small, swirled rosettes. You can also pipe it in 1 large spiral, starting at the outside edge of the

tart and working in. If you don't have a pastry bag, carefully spread on the meringue with a spatula, making a 2-inch-high topping finished with artistic swirls. Bake in the center of the oven for 8 to 10 minutes, just until the peaks of the meringue are golden brown. Cool on a wire rack. This tart is best served within a few hours of baking. SERVES 8

Tarte au fromage blanc Les Alisiers

LES ALISIERS' ALSATIAN CHEESECAKE

For the Tart

- 1 RECIPE PÂTE FEUILLETÉE RAPIDE (PAGE 21),
  OR 2 SHEETS COMMERCIAL PUFF PASTRY,
  OR 1 RECIPE PÂTE BRISÉE AU SUCRE (PAGE 17),
  CHILLED BUT NOT FROZEN

- 2 POUNDS FROMAGE BLANC, OR 1 POUND
  EACH RICOTTA CHEESE AND CREAM CHEESE

- 4 LARGE EGGS, SEPARATED

- JUICE AND GRATED ZEST OF 1/2 LARGE LEMON

- 1 TEASPOON VANILLA EXTRACT

- 1 TABLESPOON ALL-PURPOSE FLOUR

- 1 TABLESPOON CORNSTARCH

- 3/4 CUP GRANULATED SUGAR

- 2 TABLESPOONS CONFECTIONERS' SUGAR

For the Raspberry Coulis

- 1 PINT RASPBERRIES

- 2 TABLESPOONS CONFECTIONERS' SUGAR

If you travel through the verdant wine country of Alsace, along the winding Route du Vin, chances are you will encounter the *tarte au fromage blanc* almost daily, in the windows of village bakeshops and on the menus of cozy country inns. The recipe for this tangy Alsatian cheesecake, made with the region's silky, unctuous *fromage blanc*, comes from Ella Degouy, owner of the delightful hilltop auberge, Les Alisiers, in Lapoutroie, where the *tarte au fromage blanc* is a perennial favorite. In the absence of *fromage blanc*, you can make this tart with a combination of whipped ricotta and cream cheese. But make the effort to obtain *fromage blanc*, available by mail order in regular and fat-free varieties (see page 125)—the real thing is better!

Note: If you make this tart with fat-free *fromage blanc*, the filling will be somewhat less creamy, but you will have a fat-free cheesecake, apart from the crust. For a truly fat-free dessert, I occasionally make just the cheesecake filling, baking it in a greased soufflé dish and serving it with the raspberry coulis in the recipe. *Voilà*, Mousse au Fromage Blanc!

To make the tart: Roll out the pastry on a floured surface to a 14-inch circle about ⅛-inch thick. Transfer it immediately to a buttered 9-inch springform pan, pressing it carefully into the bottom and up the sides. Trim the excess dough, cover with plastic wrap, and chill.

Preheat the oven to 400°F.

In a large mixing bowl, combine the *fromage blanc*, egg yolks, lemon juice, zest, vanilla extract, flour, cornstarch, and granulated sugar. Whisk briskly until smooth. In a separate bowl, beat the egg whites just until they form stiff peaks. Using a rubber spatula, gently fold the egg whites into the cheese mixture. Fill the pastry shell with the mixture and set on the center rack of the oven. Bake for 30 minutes.

Remove tart from the oven and run a metal spatula or a small sharp knife around the sides of the pan to prevent sticking, then make a shallow (about ½-inch) horizontal cut into the filling above the crust all the way around the tart to vent the steam. Reduce the oven temperature to 350°F and continue baking another 30 to 40 minutes, until the filling has set and the top has browned. (If the top becomes too brown before the filling has set, cover the surface lightly with aluminum foil and continue baking.) Reverse the tart pan and set on a wire rack to cool upside down.

When tart is cool, turn pan right side up. Unmold the tart, removing the sides but leaving the bottom in place, arrange on a serving dish, and sprinkle with confectioners' sugar.

To make the raspberry coulis: Puree the raspberries with the sugar in a blender or food processor, then strain. Chill until ready to serve.

Serve tart at room temperature or chilled, with raspberry coulis drizzled around each slice. SERVES 6 TO 8

Tourte aux blettes

MEDITERRANEAN SWISS CHARD TART

- 1 10 1/2-INCH PÂTE SABLÉE SHELL (PAGE 18), PARTIALLY BAKED, AND 1 11-INCH CIRCLE OF DOUGH TO COVER, CHILLED

- 1/2 CUP RAISINS

- 1/4 CUP DARK RUM

- 2 POUNDS SWISS CHARD

- 2 GRANNY SMITH APPLES, PEELED, CORED, AND DICED SMALL

- 1 CUP CRÈME PÂTISSIÈRE (PAGE 23)

- 1/2 CUP PINE NUTS, TOASTED

- 1/4 CUP APRICOT JAM GLAZE (PAGE 26)

- 3 TABLESPOONS SUGAR

This unusual dessert tart—a sweet confection made with the leaves of Swiss chard, a vegetable in the beet family—is a traditional treat from the Mediterranean town of Nice. A savory version exists as well, but it's the sweet Swiss chard tart that is the real surprise. The chard in combination with pine nuts, raisins, apples, and pastry cream forms a filling vaguely reminiscent of mincemeat, and is absolutely delicious. This recipe comes compliments of Guy Payard, owner of Nice's port-side *pâtisserie* Au Nid des Friandises and father of notable pastry chef François Payard of New York's Restaurant Daniel.

The night before preparing the tart, combine the raisins and rum in a small bowl, cover, and reserve until ready to use.

Preheat the oven to 375°F.

Strip the green portion of the chard leaves from the thick white stalks, discarding the stalks. Chop the chard coarsely, then blanch for 3 minutes in a pot of boiling water; drain and set aside. In a medium bowl, combine the apples and pastry cream, folding with a rubber spatula to mix. Fold in the pine nuts. Drain the raisins and fold them in, then fold in the Swiss chard.

Spoon the filling into the tart shell. Cover with the circle of dough, pressing the edges together to seal. Using a sharp knife, cut several slits in the crust for ventilation. Bake for 40 to 45 minutes, until the crust is an even golden brown and feels firm in the center. Set tart on a wire rack to cool. Brush with glaze, sprinkle with sugar, and serve at room temperature. SERVES 6 TO 8

Tarte au riz à l'impératrice

RICE À L'IMPÉRATRICE TART

For the Tart

- 1 10 1/2-INCH PÂTE SABLÉE SHELL (PAGE 18), PARTIALLY BAKED, WITH 1 TEASPOON VANILLA EXTRACT ADDED TO THE DOUGH ALONG WITH THE EGGS
- 1/2 CUP RAISINS
- 1/4 CUP DARK RUM
- 4 CUPS MILK
- 1/4 CUP SUGAR
- 1/2 CUP LONG-GRAIN RICE
- 4 LARGE EGG YOLKS
- 12 TABLESPOONS (1 1/2 STICKS) UNSALTED BUTTER, CUT INTO BITS
- 2 VANILLA BEANS OR 1 TEASPOON VANILLA EXTRACT

For the Glazed Apples

- 8 GRANNY SMITH APPLES, PEELED, CORED, AND CUT INTO 8 SEGMENTS
- 1/2 CUP (1 STICK) UNSALTED BUTTER, SOFTENED
- 1 CUP SUGAR
- 1/2 CUP APRICOT JAM GLAZE (PAGE 26), SLIGHTLY WARMED

Among the many pleasures of dining at New York's Restaurant Daniel are the memorable desserts created by *pâtissier* François Payard. In his repertoire of inspired desserts is this rich, creamy rice tart topped with glazed apples—a variation on the classic French rice-and-custard dessert, *riz à l'impératrice*. The preparation of this tart requires some extra effort, but the results are impressive.

To make the tart: Combine the raisins and rum in a small bowl, cover, and let soak overnight, or at least 5 hours.

Preheat the oven to 350°F.

In a medium saucepan, combine the milk and sugar. Bring to a boil, then add the rice. Simmer about 14 minutes, until rice is cooked. Reduce the heat under the rice to medium low, then stir in the egg yolks. Stir constantly, until the mixture is slightly thickened and coats the back of the spoon. Add the butter and vanilla, and stir to blend. Drain the raisins and add them to the rice mixture, stirring to blend.

Pour the rice mixture into the crust. Bake for 15 to 20 minutes, until the creamy center of the tart is set. Remove and place on a wire rack. While the tart is still hot, brush on a layer of apricot glaze. Cool.

To make the glazed apples: Heat the oven to 375°F. Arrange the apple slices on a baking sheet. Brush them with the softened butter and sprinkle with the sugar. Bake for about 15 minutes, until the apples are just tender. Set on a wire rack to cool. Arrange the apples in a spiral design on top of the tart, starting with the outside edge and working in. Brush a layer of apricot glaze over the apples, and let set for at least 1 hour. Serve at room temperature or chilled. SERVES 8

Note: According to François Payard, you can adapt this tart to any time of the year by substituting the best-tasting fruit of the season, such as pears, peaches, or apricots, for the apples in the topping.

CONVERSIONS

WEIGHT EQUIVALENTS

The metric weights given in this chart are not exact equivalents, but have been rounded up or down slightly to make measuring easier.

Avoirdupois	Metric
¼ oz	7 g
½ oz	15 g
1 oz	30 g
2 oz	60 g
3 oz	90 g
4 oz	115 g
5 oz	150 g
6 oz	175 g
7 oz	200 g
8 oz (½ lb)	225 g
9 oz	250 g
10 oz	300 g
11 oz	325 g
12 oz	350 g
13 oz	375 g
14 oz	400 g
15 oz	425 g
16 oz (1 lb)	450 g
1 lb 2 oz	500 g
1½ lb	750 g
2 lb	900 g
2½ lb	1 kg
3 lb	1.4 kg
4 lb	1.8 kg
4½ lb	2 kg

VOLUME EQUIVALENTS

These are not exact equivalents for the American cups and spoons, but have been rounded up or down slightly to make measuring easier.

American	Metric	Imperial
¼ t	1.25 ml	
½ t	2.5 ml	
1 t	5 ml	
½ T (1½ t)	7.5 ml	
1 T (3 t)	15 ml	
¼ cup (4 T)	60 ml	2 fl. oz
⅓ cup (5 T)	75 ml	2½ fl oz
½ cup (8 T)	125 ml	4 fl oz
⅔ cup (10 T)	150 ml	5 fl oz (¼ pint)
¾ cup (12 T)	175 ml	6 fl oz (⅓ pint)
1 cup (16 T)	250 ml	8 fl oz
1¼ cups	300 ml	10 fl oz (½ pint)
1½ cups	350 ml	12 fl oz
1 pint (2 cups)	500 ml	16 fl oz
2½ cups	575 ml	20 fl oz (1 pint)
1 quart (4 cups)	1 litre	1¾ pints

OVEN TEMPERATURE EQUIVALENTS

Oven	°F.	°C.	Gas Mark
very cool	250–275	130–140	½–1
cool	300	150	2
warm	325	170	3
moderate	350	180	4
moderately hot	375	190	5
	400	200	6
hot	425	220	7
very hot	450	230	8
	475	250	9

Appendix

A Guide to Featured Hotels, Restaurants,
Tearooms, Pâtisseries, and Wineries:

HOTELS

Château de Blanville
Saint Luperce
28190 Courville-sur-Eure, France
Tel: (011-33) 2-37-26-77-36
Fax: (011-33) 2-37-26-78-02

Château des Briottières
49330 Champigné, France
Tel: (011-33) 2-41-42-00-02
Fax: (011-33) 2-41-42-01-55

Château du Domaine Saint-Martin
Route de Coursegoules
06140 Vence, France
Tel: (011-33) 4-93-58-02-02
Fax: (011-33) 4-93-24-08-91

Hostellerie Bérard
83740 La Cadière d'Azur, France
Tel: (011-33) 4-94-90-11-43
Fax: (011-33) 4-94-90-01-94

Hostellerie Le Cerf
30 rue Gal-de-Gal
67520 Marlenheim, France
Tel: (011-33) 3-88-87-73-73
Fax: (011-33) 3-88-87-68-08

Hôtel Le Parc
55-57 avenue Raymond-Poincaré
75116 Paris, France
Tel: (011-33) 1-44-05-66-66
Fax: (011-33) 1-44-05-66-00

La Côte d'Or
2 rue Argentine
21210 Saulieu, France
Tel: (011-33) 3-80-64-07-66
Fax: (011-33) 3-80-64-08-92

La Réserve de Beaulieu
5 boulevard Gal-Leclerc
06310 Beaulieu-sur-Mer, France
Tel: (011-33) 4-93-01-00-01
Fax: (011-33) 4-93-01-28-99

Le Mas du Langoustier
83400 Ile de Porquerolles, France
Tel: (011-33) 4-94-58-30-09
Fax: (011-33) 4-94-58-36-02

Les Alisiers
5 rue Faude
68650 Lapoutroie, France
Tel: (011-33) 3-89-87-52-82
Fax: (011-33) 3-89-47-22-38

RESTAURANTS

Bistro d'à Coté
10 rue Gustave-Flaubert
75017 Paris, France
Tel: (011-33) 1-42-67-05-81
Fax: (011-33) 1-47-63-82-75

Le Louis XV
Hôtel de Paris
Place de Casino
98000 Monte Carlo, Monaco
Tel: (011-377) 92-16-68-17
Fax: (011-377) 92-16-69-21

Les Célébrités
Essex House
155 West 58th Street
New York, New York 10021
Tel: 212-484-5113

Michel Rostang
20 rue Rennequin
75017 Paris, France
Tel: (011-33) 1-47-63-40-77
Fax: (011-33) 1-47-63-82-75

Restaurant Daniel
20 East 76th Street
New York, New York 10022
Tel: 212-288-0033

TEAROOMS AND PÂTISSERIES

Au Nid des Friandises
18 rue Barla
06300 Nice, France
Tel: (011-33) 4-93-55-37-74

Cador
2 rue de l'Amiral de Coligny
75001 Paris, France
Tel: (011-33) 1-45-08-19-18

Jean-Luc Poujauran
20 rue Jean-Nicot
75007 Paris, France
Tel: (011-33) 1-47-05-80-88

La Flûte Gana
226 rue des Pyrénées
75020 Paris, France
Tel: (011-33) 1-43-58-42-62

Les Nuits des Thés
22 rue de Beaune
75007 Paris, France
Tel: (011-33) 1-47-03-92-07

Gérard Mulot
76 rue de Seine
75006 Paris, France
Tel: (011-33) 1-43-26-85-77

WINERIES

Château Lamothe
Haux
33550 Langoiran, France
Tel: (011-33) 5-56-23-05-07
Fax: (011-33) 5-56-23-24-49

Domaine de Lagrezette
46140 Caillac, France
Tel: (011-33) 5-65-20-07-42
Fax: (011-33) 5-65-20-06-95

MAIL-ORDER KITCHEN EQUIPMENT AND BAKEWARE SUPPLY HOUSES

Bridge Kitchenware Corporation
214 East 52nd Street
New York, New York 10022
New York store telephone:
212-688-4220
Catalog information and customer service:
212-838-6746

Charles Lamalle
36 West 25th Street, 6th floor
New York, New York 10036
Tel: 212-242-0750

King Arthur Flour Baker's Catalog
Box 876
Norwich, Vermont 05055
Tel: 800-827-6836

MAIL-ORDER SPECIALTY INGREDIENTS AND FOOD SOURCES

For fine bread and pastry flours, contact the following suppliers for information or a catalog:

Arrowhead Mills
Box 866
Hereford, Texas 79045
Tel: 806-364-0730

Great Valley Mills
687 Mill Road
Telford, Pennsylvania 18969
Tel: 215-754-7800

Walnut Acres
Penns Creek, Pennsylvania 17862
Tel: 800-433-3998 or 717-837-0601

For a wide variety of specialty ingredients, including vanilla sugar, Valrhona bulk chocolate, vanilla beans, cocoa powder, fine olive oils, olive paste, and vinegars, contact the following companies for information or a catalog:

Balducci's
424 Avenue of the Americas
New York, New York 10011
Tel: 800-822-1444 or 212-673-2600

Dean & Deluca
560 Broadway
New York, New York 10012
Tel: 800-221-7714 or 212-431-1691

Maid of Scandinavia
3244 Raleigh Avenue
Minneapolis, Minnesota 55461
Tel: 800-328-6722 or 512-927-7966

For excellent crème fraîche, fromage blanc, and other specialty dairy products:

Vermont Butter and Cheese Company
P.O. Box 95
Websterville, Vermont 05678
Tel: 800-884-6287 or 802-479-9371

For a selection of goat cheese—fresh, aged, or herbed:

Little Rainbow Chèvre
Box 379 Rodham Road
Hillsdale, New York 12529
Tel: 518-325-3351

For domestic foie gras, fresh ducks, tasty terrines, pâtés, and prepared entrees:

D'Artagnan
399 St. Paul Avenue
Jersey City, New Jersey 07306
Tel: 800-DARTAGNAN

For smoked eastern and western salmon:

Ducktrap River Fish Farm
RFD #2 Box 378
Lincolnville, Maine 04849
Tel: 207-763-3960

PARIS KITCHEN AND TABLEWARE
SUPPLY COMPANIES

If you're visiting Paris, be sure to drop in to several of these professional kitchen and restaurant stores that also sell retail to consumers. The range of merchandise will amaze you. On request, most vendors will pack your purchases securely for you to carry back, but will not ship overseas:

A. Simon
36 rue Etienne-Marcel
75002 Paris, France
Tel: (011-33) 1-42-33-71-65 (open Mon.–Sat.)

Dehillerin
18-20 rue Coquillière
75001 Paris, France
Tel: (011-33) 1-42-36-53-13 (open Mon.–Sat.)

MORA et Cie
13 rue Montmartre
75001 Paris, France
Tel: (011-33) 1-45-08-19-24 (open Mon.–Fri.)

Verrerie des Halles
15 rue du Louvre
75001 Paris, France
Tel: (011-33) 1-42-36-86-02 (open Mon.–Sat.)

For antique French table linens, bakeware, and kitchen collectibles, as well as charming contemporary tableware, cookbooks, and linens:

Au Bain Marie
10 rue Boissy-d'Anglas
75008 Paris, France
Tel: (011-33) 1-42-66-59-74 (open Mon.–Sat.)

Note: When phoning France from within the United States, dial number as listed; when phoning from within France, drop the international (011) and country (33) codes, and add a "0" before the area code (ie: "01-" for Paris; "04-" for Nice).

Index

(Page numbers in *italic* refer to photographs.)